HARRY S. TRUMAN

HARRY S. TRUMAN

J. Perry Leavell, Jr.

CHELSEA HOUSE PUBLISHERS
NEW YORK
NEW HAVEN   PHILADELPHIA

EDITOR-IN-CHIEF: Nancy Toff
EXECUTIVE EDITOR: Remmel T. Nunn
MANAGING EDITOR: Karyn Gullen Browne
COPY CHIEF: Juliann Barbato
PICTURE EDITOR: Adrian G. Allen
ART DIRECTOR: Giannella Garrett
MANUFACTURING MANAGER: Gerald Levine

Staff for TRUMAN:

SENIOR EDITOR: John W. Selfridge
ASSISTANT EDITOR: Sean Dolan
EDITORIAL ASSISTANT: David Wm. Gibson
COPY EDITORS: James Guiry, Ellen Scordato
ASSOCIATE PICTURE EDITOR: Juliette Dickstein
PICTURE RESEARCHER: Cheryl Moch
SENIOR DESIGNER: Teresa Clark
ASSISTANT DESIGNER: Jill Goldreyer
PRODUCTION COORDINATOR: Joseph Romano
COVER ILLUSTRATION: Robin Peterson

CREATIVE DIRECTOR: Harold Steinberg

Frontispiece courtesy of AP/Wide World Photos

First Printing

1 3 5 7 9 8 6 4 2

Library of Congress Cataloging in Publication Data

Leavell, J. Perry, Jr. HARRY S. TRUMAN

(World leaders past & present)
Bibliography: p.
1. Truman, Harry S., 1884–1972—Juvenile literature.
2. Presidents—United States—Biography—Juvenile
literature. [1. Truman, Harry S., 1884–1972.
2. Presidents] I. Title. II. Series: World leaders past &
present.
E814.L43   1988   973.918′092′4 [B] [92]   87-18395

ISBN 0-87754-558-8

Contents

CHELSEA HOUSE PUBLISHERS

WORLD LEADERS PAST & PRESENT

ADENAUER
ALEXANDER THE GREAT
MARC ANTONY
KING ARTHUR
ATATÜRK
ATTLEE
BEGIN
BEN-GURION
BISMARCK
LÉON BLUM
BOLÍVAR
CESARE BORGIA
BRANDT
BREZHNEV
CAESAR
CALVIN
CASTRO
CATHERINE THE GREAT
CHARLEMAGNE
CHIANG KAI-SHEK
CHURCHILL
CLEMENCEAU
CLEOPATRA
CORTÉS
CROMWELL
DANTON
DE GAULLE
DE VALERA
DISRAELI
EISENHOWER
ELEANOR OF AQUITAINE
QUEEN ELIZABETH I
FERDINAND AND ISABELLA
FRANCO

FREDERICK THE GREAT
INDIRA GANDHI
MOHANDAS GANDHI
GARIBALDI
GENGHIS KHAN
GLADSTONE
GORBACHEV
HAMMARSKJÖLD
HENRY VIII
HENRY OF NAVARRE
HINDENBURG
HITLER
HO CHI MINH
HUSSEIN
IVAN THE TERRIBLE
ANDREW JACKSON
JEFFERSON
JOAN OF ARC
POPE JOHN XXIII
LYNDON JOHNSON
JUÁREZ
JOHN F. KENNEDY
KENYATTA
KHOMEINI
KHRUSHCHEV
MARTIN LUTHER KING, JR.
KISSINGER
LENIN
LINCOLN
LLOYD GEORGE
LOUIS XIV
LUTHER
JUDAS MACCABEUS
MAO ZEDONG

MARY, QUEEN OF SCOTS
GOLDA MEIR
METTERNICH
MUSSOLINI
NAPOLEON
NASSER
NEHRU
NERO
NICHOLAS II
NIXON
NKRUMAH
PERICLES
PERÓN
QADDAFI
ROBESPIERRE
ELEANOR ROOSEVELT
FRANKLIN D. ROOSEVELT
THEODORE ROOSEVELT
SADAT
STALIN
SUN YAT-SEN
TAMERLANE
THATCHER
TITO
TROTSKY
TRUDEAU
TRUMAN
VICTORIA
WASHINGTON
WEIZMANN
WOODROW WILSON
XERXES
ZHOU ENLAI

ON LEADERSHIP
Arthur M. Schlesinger, jr.

LEADERSHIP, it may be said, is really what makes the world go round. Love no doubt smooths the passage; but love is a private transaction between consenting adults. Leadership is a public transaction with history. The idea of leadership affirms the capacity of individuals to move, inspire, and mobilize masses of people so that they act together in pursuit of an end. Sometimes leadership serves good purposes, sometimes bad; but whether the end is benign or evil, great leaders are those men and women who leave their personal stamp on history.

Now, the very concept of leadership implies the proposition that individuals can make a difference. This proposition has never been universally accepted. From classical times to the present day, eminent thinkers have regarded individuals as no more than the agents and pawns of larger forces, whether the gods and goddesses of the ancient world or, in the modern era, race, class, nation, the dialectic, the will of the people, the spirit of the times, history itself. Against such forces, the individual dwindles into insignificance.

So contends the thesis of historical determinism. Tolstoy's great novel *War and Peace* offers a famous statement of the case. Why, Tolstoy asked, did millions of men in the Napoleonic wars, denying their human feelings and their common sense, move back and forth across Europe slaughtering their fellows? "The war," Tolstoy answered, "was bound to happen simply because it was bound to happen." All prior history predetermined it. As for leaders, they, Tolstoy said, "are but the labels that serve to give a name to an end and, like labels, they have the least possible connection with the event." The greater the leader, "the more conspicuous the inevitability and the predestination of every act he commits." The leader, said Tolstoy, is "the slave of history."

Determinism takes many forms. Marxism is the determinism of class. Nazism the determinism of race. But the idea of men and women as the slaves of history runs athwart the deepest human instincts. Rigid determinism abolishes the idea of human freedom—

the assumption of free choice that underlies every move we make, every word we speak, every thought we think. It abolishes the idea of human responsibility, since it is manifestly unfair to reward or punish people for actions that are by definition beyond their control. No one can live consistently by any deterministic creed. The Marxist states prove this themselves by their extreme susceptibility to the cult of leadership.

More than that, history refutes the idea that individuals make no difference. In December 1931 a British politician crossing Park Avenue in New York City between 76th and 77th Streets around 10:30 P.M. looked in the wrong direction and was knocked down by an automobile—a moment, he later recalled, of a man aghast, a world aglare: "I do not understand why I was not broken like an eggshell or squashed like a gooseberry." Fourteen months later an American politician, sitting in an open car in Miami, Florida, was fired on by an assassin; the man beside him was hit. Those who believe that individuals make no difference to history might well ponder whether the next two decades would have been the same had Mario Constasino's car killed Winston Churchill in 1931 and Giuseppe Zangara's bullet killed Franklin Roosevelt in 1933. Suppose, in addition, that Adolf Hitler had been killed in the street fighting during the Munich *Putsch* of 1923 and that Lenin had died of typhus during World War I. What would the 20th century be like now?

For better or for worse, individuals do make a difference. "The notion that a people can run itself and its affairs anonymously," wrote the philosopher William James, "is now well known to be the silliest of absurdities. Mankind does nothing save through initiatives on the part of inventors, great or small, and imitation by the rest of us—these are the sole factors in human progress. Individuals of genius show the way, and set the patterns, which common people then adopt and follow."

Leadership, James suggests, means leadership in thought as well as in action. In the long run, leaders in thought may well make the greater difference to the world. But, as Woodrow Wilson once said, "Those only are leaders of men, in the general eye, who lead in action. . . . It is at their hands that new thought gets its translation into the crude language of deeds." Leaders in thought often invent in solitude and obscurity, leaving to later generations the tasks of imitation. Leaders in action—the leaders portrayed in this series—have to be effective in their own time.

And they cannot be effective by themselves. They must act in response to the rhythms of their age. Their genius must be adapted, in a phrase of William James's, "to the receptivities of the moment." Leaders are useless without followers. "There goes the mob," said the French politician hearing a clamor in the streets. "I am their leader. I must follow them." Great leaders turn the inchoate emotions of the mob to purposes of their own. They seize on the opportunities of their time, the hopes, fears, frustrations, crises, potentialities. They succeed when events have prepared the way for them, when the community is awaiting to be aroused, when they can provide the clarifying and organizing ideas. Leadership ignites the circuit between the individual and the mass and thereby alters history.

It may alter history for better or for worse. Leaders have been responsible for the most extravagant follies and most monstrous crimes that have beset suffering humanity. They have also been vital in such gains as humanity has made in individual freedom, religious and racial tolerance, social justice and respect for human rights.

There is no sure way to tell in advance who is going to lead for good and who for evil. But a glance at the gallery of men and women in *World Leaders—Past and Present* suggests some useful tests.

One test is this: do leaders lead by force or by persuasion? By command or by consent? Through most of history leadership was exercised by the divine right of authority. The duty of followers was to defer and to obey. "Theirs not to reason why,/ Theirs but to do and die." On occasion, as with the so-called "enlightened despots" of the 18th century in Europe, absolutist leadership was animated by humane purposes. More often, absolutism nourished the passion for domination, land, gold and conquest and resulted in tyranny.

The great revolution of modern times has been the revolution of equality. The idea that all people should be equal in their legal condition has undermined the old structure of authority, hierarchy and deference. The revolution of equality has had two contrary effects on the nature of leadership. For equality, as Alexis de Tocqueville pointed out in his great study *Democracy in America*, might mean equality in servitude as well as equality in freedom.

"I know of only two methods of establishing equality in the political world," Tocqueville wrote. "Rights must be given to every citizen, or none at all to anyone . . . save one, who is the master of all." There was no middle ground "between the sovereignty of all and the absolute power of one man." In his astonishing prediction of 20th-century totalitarian dictatorship, Tocqueville explained how the revolution of equality could lead to the *"Führerprinzip"* and more terrible absolutism than the world had ever known.

But when rights are given to every citizen and the sovereignty of all is established, the problem of leadership takes a new form, becomes more exacting than ever before. It is easy to issue commands and enforce them by the rope and the stake, the concentration camp and the *gulag.* It is much harder to use argument and achievement to overcome opposition and win consent. The Founding Fathers of the United States understood the difficulty. They believed that history had given them the opportunity to decide, as Alexander Hamilton wrote in the first Federalist Paper, whether men are indeed capable of basing government on "reflection and choice, or whether they are forever destined to depend . . . on accident and force."

Government by reflection and choice called for a new style of leadership and a new quality of followership. It required leaders to be responsive to popular concerns, and it required followers to be active and informed participants in the process. Democracy does not eliminate emotion from politics; sometimes it fosters demagoguery; but it is confident that, as the greatest of democratic leaders put it, you cannot fool all of the people all of the time. It measures leadership by results and retires those who overreach or falter or fail.

It is true that in the long run despots are measured by results too. But they can postpone the day of judgment, sometimes indefinitely, and in the meantime they can do infinite harm. It is also true that democracy is no guarantee of virtue and intelligence in government, for the voice of the people is not necessarily the voice of God. But democracy, by assuring the right of opposition, offers built-in resistance to the evils inherent in absolutism. As the theologian Reinhold Niebuhr summed it up, "Man's capacity for justice makes democracy possible, but man's inclination to injustice makes democracy necessary."

A second test for leadership is the end for which power is sought. When leaders have as their goal the supremacy of a master race or the promotion of totalitarian revolution or the acquisition and exploitation of colonies or the protection of greed and privilege or the preservation of personal power, it is likely that their leadership will do little to advance the cause of humanity. When their goal is the abolition of slavery, the liberation of women, the enlargement of opportunity for the poor and powerless, the extension of equal rights to racial minorities, the defense of the freedoms of expression and opposition, it is likely that their leadership will increase the sum of human liberty and welfare.

Leaders have done great harm to the world. They have also conferred great benefits. You will find both sorts in this series. Even "good" leaders must be regarded with a certain wariness. Leaders are not demigods; they put on their trousers one leg after another just like ordinary mortals. No leader is infallible, and every leader needs to be reminded of this at regular intervals. Irreverence irritates leaders but is their salvation. Unquestioning submission corrupts leaders and demands followers. Making a cult of a leader is always a mistake. Fortunately hero worship generates its own antidote. "Every hero," said Emerson, "becomes a bore at last."

The signal benefit the great leaders confer is to embolden the rest of us to live according to our own best selves, to be active, insistent, and resolute in affirming our own sense of things. For great leaders attest to the reality of human freedom against the supposed inevitabilities of history. And they attest to the wisdom and power that may lie within the most unlikely of us, which is why Abraham Lincoln remains the supreme example of great leadership. A great leader, said Emerson, exhibits new possibilities to all humanity. "We feed on genius. . . . Great men exist that there may be greater men."

Great leaders, in short, justify themselves by emancipating and empowering their followers. So humanity struggles to master its destiny, remembering with Alexis de Tocqueville: "It is true that around every man a fatal circle is traced beyond which he cannot pass; but within the wide verge of that circle he is powerful and free; as it is with man, so with communities."

1

A Leader of the Atomic Age

Early in the morning of August 6, 1945, three American B-29 bombers flew north from the tiny Pacific island of Tinian toward the Japanese city of Hiroshima. The 1,500-mile trip took six and a half hours; the lead pilot later called it "the dullest trip anyone ever took."

One plane, the *Enola Gay*, commanded by Lieutenant Colonel Paul W. Tibbets, Jr., carried an atomic bomb. Two escort planes flew behind to measure and record the explosion's impact. The bomb was squat and ugly, 10 feet long and 28 inches in diameter. Crew members had written messages on its side as if it were a cast on a broken leg: "To Hell with the Emperor" and "This is for the boys on the *Indianapolis*."

Halfway to Hiroshima, the three planes passed over the island of Iwo Jima, which five months earlier had been the site of a bloody battle between the Japanese and the Americans. The Japanese had fought fiercely to repel the American invasion, knowing that Iwo Jima would become one more island air base from which the Americans would launch devastating bombing raids on Japanese cities.

The world has achieved brilliance without conscience. Ours is a world of nuclear giants and ethical infants.
—GEN. OMAR N. BRADLEY
Armistice Day address, 1948

Harry S. Truman became the 33rd president of the United States upon the death of Franklin Roosevelt in April 1945. After less than four months in office, Truman was faced with one of the most difficult and controversial decisions ever to confront a U.S. president: whether to drop the atom bomb on Japan to end World War II.

More than 20,000 Japanese troops had barricaded themselves in bunkers protected by thick concrete walls from which machine guns and artillery could strafe every yard of the island. The bunkers were connected by miles of underground tunnels. For 74 consecutive days, American ships and planes bombarded the island. Then, on February 19, 1945, the marines landed. Despite unbelievably brutal fighting, the Japanese refused to surrender. More than 20,000 Japanese troops were killed; only 218 were captured alive. The marines suffered the worst casualties in their history: 6,821 were killed in less than a month, and more than 18,000 were wounded. Now, five months later, the three bombers formed a tighter formation above the desolate island and continued their flight northward.

Fifty miles from the Japanese coast, the crew received a radio message confirming that the weather was clear over Hiroshima. Two hundred forty-five thousand people lived there, between the green hills and the waters of the Inland Sea. For weeks now, the huge B-29s had flown over the city every day on their daily bombing runs, but Hiroshima had thus far been spared a major bombing. Local citizens discussed their good luck; according to one story, President Truman's mother was said to live nearby, protecting the city from the fury of the American planes.

As they neared the target, one of the planes dropped back in order to photograph the bombing. A second dropped instrument packages that would seek scientific evidence of the bomb's power. The *Enola Gay* released the bomb, the plane jerking upward as the 9,000-pound weight tumbled free. The planes immediately changed direction in order to put as much distance between them and the explosion as possible. The crew, in specially designed goggles, waited for a tense 43 seconds.

Two thousand feet above the city the bomb exploded. The crews on the three planes, now several miles away, looked backward and saw the city disappear. A huge multicolored cloud of smoke rose in the sky miles above the city and continued to be visible after the planes had flown 250 miles. Mo-

The U.S. Marines landing on Iwo Jima, a small volcanic island 700 miles south of Tokyo, in February 1945 met a large Japanese force entrenched in caves and tunnels. The brutal fighting that followed convinced the Roosevelt administration that an invasion of the Japanese home islands would encounter fierce resistance.

Lieutenant Colonel Paul W. Tibbets (center) with the crew of the *Enola Gay*. Tibbets commanded the mission that released the atom bomb on Hiroshima on August 6, 1945, ushering the world into the nuclear age.

ments later Tibbets composed a crisp military report: "Results clear-cut, successful in all respects. Visible effects greater than in any test. Conditions normal in airplane following delivery." Later, back at the officers' club on Tinian, he described the mission even more succinctly: "Saw city, destroyed same."

Three days later one of the crews flew another B-29 bomber, *Bock's Car*, toward the Japanese mainland. Major Charles W. Sweeney and his crew carried a different kind of bomb — plutonium rather than uranium. Called "Fat Man," the plutonium bomb was larger than the "Little Boy" dropped on Hiroshima.

The primary target was Kokura (now Kitakyushu), but clouds protected the city from the eyes of the bombers. So the plane turned toward Nagasaki, a city overlooking the East China Sea. At 11:01 A.M. on August 9, 1945, the second bomb was dropped. The men on *Bock's Car*, seeing their second atomic explosion in three days, were awed. An assistant flight engineer later described his feelings thus: "I

A mushroom cloud billows over Nagasaki after the second atomic bomb was dropped there on August 9. The decision to use a second bomb, in order to impress upon the Japanese that the United States could develop more than one, had been made during the Roosevelt administration.

thought maybe the world had come to an end, and we'd caused it."

The men who were astounded by the large mushroom cloud the bomb's detonation produced did not see through it to the carnage on the ground. Seventy thousand Japanese were killed and an equal number seriously wounded in Hiroshima; perhaps 40,000 more died at Nagasaki, with another 60,000 wounded. Still unknown to the victims were the horrors of radiation, which would stretch ahead and maim and mutilate future generations. The American critic Dwight Macdonald realized that the dropping of the atom bombs ushered in a new era; the very "concepts [of] 'war' and 'progress,'" he declared, "are now obsolete."

The man who made the final decision to drop the atomic bombs was the president of the United States, Harry S. Truman. He had become president less than four months before, on April 12, 1945, when Franklin Delano Roosevelt died. A year earlier,

The rubble and debris of Nagasaki following the explosion of the atom bomb. More than one-third of the city was destroyed by the blast, and nearly 100,000 citizens were killed or wounded.

when he was a senator, he had learned of the existence of a large-scale secret military project, called the Manhattan Project, but he did not know its significance. Later, when he became vice-president, he was told by Roosevelt during a photo session of the development of a powerful new bomb, but it was only after he became president that Truman learned the full details. On April 25, 1945, Secretary of War Henry Stimson proposed the creation of a special committee to advise Stimson and the president on the use of the new weapon.

This special group, known as the Interim Committee, met three times to consider the role of the atomic bomb in American policy. Its members included Stimson, representatives of the State and Navy departments, the presidents of Harvard University and the Massachusetts Institute of Technology, and the master scientist who directed the building of the bomb, J. Robert Oppenheimer.

One member of the Interim Committee later wrote, "It seemed to be a foregone conclusion that the bomb would be used. It was regarding only the

Hiroshima after the atom bomb. Ninety percent of the city was destroyed and 140,000 people were killed or wounded.

Truman (center) met with British prime minister Winston Churchill (left) and Soviet leader Joseph Stalin (right) at Potsdam, Germany, in July 1945 to discuss the occupation of postwar Germany. At Potsdam Truman told Stalin that the United States had developed a "new weapon of unusual destructive force."

details of strategy and tactics that differing views were expressed." Critics have argued that the explosions were not necessary, that a demonstration blast witnessed by the Japanese would have been sufficient to secure their unconditional surrender. Others disagree. Dr. Isidor I. Rabi of Columbia University, a Nobel laureate, observed at the time, "Who would they send and what would he report? You would have to tell him what instruments to bring, and where to stand, and what to measure. Otherwise it would look like a lot of pyrotechnics. It would take someone who understood the theory to realize what he was seeing. It was not a trivial point. You would have to have built a model town to make a realistic demonstration. It would require a level of communications between us and the Japanese which was inconceivable in wartime." Indeed, even after the devastation at Hiroshima and Nagasaki, some Japanese military commanders did not believe the explosions had been the result of a new weapon and urged the emperor to continue the war. On June 1, the committee unanimously recommended that the bomb be used as soon as possible, without prior warning, against a target that would show its strength. The choice of a target was left to the president.

To that point the discussions had been theoretical, for even the scientists were not sure that the bomb would work. On July 16, 1945, a test bomb was successfully exploded in the desert at Alamogordo, New Mexico. At the time, Truman was in Potsdam, Germany, meeting with the Allied leaders Joseph Stalin of the Soviet Union and Winston Churchill of Great Britain to discuss the occupation of defeated Germany and the reconstruction of postwar Europe. One day during the conference, Truman casually strolled over to Stalin to inform him that the United States had developed a weapon of great explosive power. He did not say it was an atomic device. Stalin scarcely reacted to the news, but he sent orders back home to renew the Soviet atomic research program.

The development of the bomb presented Truman with a difficult diplomatic situation. Although

Nazism was the doctrine of German dictator Adolf Hitler (front left). It combined an aggressive, expansionist foreign policy, mystical German nationalism, and a virulent doctrine of racial purity. More than 6 million people, most of them Jews and Poles, were killed in Hitler's concentration camps.

Innocent Polish citizens are rounded up by German soldiers for transport to concentration camps. Germany's invasion of Poland in September 1939 brought declarations of war from France and Great Britain, beginning World War II.

Churchill and the British knew of the Manhattan Project (indeed, British scientists had done much of the early work on nuclear weaponry, and the Manhattan Project was in many ways a combined Anglo-U.S. effort), Roosevelt and Truman were much less trustful of their Soviet allies, who had initially signed a nonaggression pact with Adolf Hitler's Nazi Germany, the aggressor in the European war. The war had left the United States and the Soviet Union as the world's foremost powers, and the communist ideology of the Soviet Union (based on the thought of the German economic philosopher Karl Marx) and the capitalist theory of the United States were held to be in unalterable opposition, making tension between the two nations all but inevitable.

Even in the heady early days of the Allied victory in Europe, it was apparent that the United States and the Soviet Union were destined to clash over such issues as the reorganization of Germany, postwar influence in Europe, territorial ambitions and claims, war reparations, and the types of governments to be established in Eastern Europe. Although Truman, his advisers, and the Interim Committee had reached a consensus that the Soviet Union, as an ally, be informed of the atomic bomb's existence before it was used, so as to allay even greater uneasiness between the allies, it was not deemed necessary to provide the Soviets with specifics. At the time the Soviets were eager to declare war on Japan and join the Asian conflict, thus staking claims to territorial demands in Asia. The news of the successful testing of the atom bomb made it possible that the war in Asia would be over before the Soviets entered it, while the possession of a mysterious new weapon by the United States would surely give that nation a bargaining edge in future negotiations with the Soviet Union.

On July 24, Truman issued a directive to the Air Force to "deliver its first special bomb as soon as weather will permit . . . after about 3 August. . . ." The order added that "additional bombs will be delivered on the above targets as soon as made ready by the project staff." Then the United States issued

The brutality of Japan's war against China from 1937 to 1945, which was often conducted against civilian targets, is vividly illustrated in this photo of a screaming child amidst the ruins of the Shanghai train station following a Japanese bombing raid.

a formal warning to Japan to surrender immediately. "The alternative for Japan," said Truman's proclamation, "is prompt and utter destruction." When Japan rejected the ultimatum, the die was cast. "There was no alternative now," Truman observed later in his memoirs.

On August 6, Truman was aboard the SS *Augusta*, sailing back to the United States after the Potsdam Conference, when he received a message delivered by the captain. Truman read of the destruction of Hiroshima and exclaimed, "This is the greatest thing in history." A second proclamation was issued in Washington under Truman's name informing the world of the event and warning Japan to surrender immediately: "If they do not now accept our terms, they may expect a rain of ruin from the air, the like of which has never been seen on this earth."

The Japanese did not respond immediately to the threat. Indeed, Japan's military leaders still demanded a fight to the last man. Even after the second bomb was dropped on Nagasaki, they continued to oppose surrender, but the emperor, Hirohito, intervened to demand that the government accept defeat. Tentative signals were sent out to the world from Japan on August 10, and on September 2, 1945, a formal surrender was signed aboard the battleship *Missouri*. World War II was over.

In later years, Truman became sensitive to criticism of his 1945 decision. In 1959 he told students at Columbia University that he went to bed and slept soundly after his decision to use the bomb. He denied repeatedly that he ever had second thoughts about the way the war ended and about the nuclear destruction in Japan, emphasizing that the American military had been planning a massive invasion of Japan as a final assault. Knowing that the Japanese would defend their home islands with a ferocity equal to their defense of Iwo Jima, he believed that by dropping the bombs he saved the lives of at least 250,000 American soldiers.

Moreover, he felt that past experience with the Japanese justified the bombing. The Japanese had

Tokyo following U.S. bombing raids. In the spring of
1945, 2 U.S. firebombing attacks killed more than
200,000 Japanese in Tokyo and burned more than 16
square miles of the city to the ground.

proved themselves untrustworthy and uncivilized by their sneak attack on Pearl Harbor on December 7, 1941, an attack that precipitated the U.S. entrance into the war. When the general secretary of the Federal Council of Churches of Christ in America telegraphed in opposition to the dropping of the bombs, Truman responded: ". . . I was greatly disturbed over the unwarranted attack by the Japanese on Pearl Harbor and their murder of our prisoners of war. . . . When you have to deal with a beast you have to treat him as a beast. . . ."

Truman, like most Americans in 1945, was hardened by the horrors of a long war. The Japanese had slaughtered hundreds of thousands of civilians in Nanjing, China, in the 1930s; the Italians had bombed cities in Ethiopia; and the Germans had enacted unspeakable horrors on civilians throughout the war years. Both the Americans and British had bombed cities during the war, with resulting civilian casualties. Early in 1945, U.S. planes dropped 2,000 tons of napalm bombs on Tokyo, creating huge balls of fire with temperatures of 1,800 degrees Fahrenheit. Some of the crew members in the last wave of American attackers vomited when they smelled the burning flesh below. Perhaps 125,000 Japanese died. Only 10 weeks before the dropping of the atomic bomb on Hiroshima, the B-29s hit Tokyo once more, killing an estimated 83,000 more citizens.

It seems evident that the decision to use the bomb was made on the basis of providing a quick end to the war, a decision that is perhaps more easily understood given the horrors and suffering of the war's previous four years. It may be argued in hindsight that the decision to drop the bomb was made too quickly and superficially. Because the weapon was developed in secrecy, few knew of its existence; the president received advice from only a handful of people. The decision to drop the second bomb seems especially vulnerable to criticism, because it followed the first so quickly and did not give the Japanese time to arrive at a decision regarding surrender. Truman and his advisers saw only two alternatives: an invasion of Japan, which all agreed would result in an appalling number of U.S. casualties and at least a year's more combat, or the quick end to the war the bomb could provide. There was little dissent about the dropping of the bomb; it had been developed in the belief that it would be used to hasten the end of the war. The dynamics that made its deployment likely had been set in motion during the Roosevelt administration; Truman had been in office barely three months, thrust into a position of power at an extremely crucial period of U.S. history. If Truman did indeed sleep well after his decision to use the bomb, then it was undoubtedly because he regarded it as the only decision he could have made.

General Dwight D. Eisenhower (center) and other Allied officials view victims of the Nazis at the German concentration camp at Gotha. The full horrors of the Nazi death camps came to light after Germany's surrender on May 7, 1945.

2

An Average Man

Harry S. Truman was born in Lamar, Missouri, on May 8, 1884. The S stood for nothing; it was a compromise agreed upon by his parents, who had wanted to name him after their respective fathers, Solomon Young and Anderson Shippe Truman.

His father, John Truman, known as "Peanuts," was a short man who pursued a long list of trades. During his lifetime he was a farmer, a livestock dealer, a grain speculator, and a night watchman. His mother, Martha Ellen Young, was the lively, intelligent daughter of a prosperous farmer and landowner. The family moved several times when Harry was a young boy. The decision to move to Independence, Missouri, was mostly his mother's idea. College educated, she wanted her children to attend the better city schools.

Independence in 1890 was a small town of approximately 6,000 people situated about 9 miles from the larger Kansas City. Harry, with his younger brother, John Vivian, and sister, Mary Jane, spent 12 formative years there. A stable community lo-

> *Without my glasses I was blind as a bat, and to tell the truth, I was kind of a sissy.*
> —HARRY S. TRUMAN
> on his childhood popularity

Captain Harry S. Truman of the 129th Field Artillery in France during World War I. Truman believed that his military experience was instrumental in the development of his political career.

Truman's parents, Martha Ellen Young and John Anderson Truman, in 1881, three years before Harry's birth.

cated near the geographic center of the United States, Independence would always be the spiritual hometown of Harry Truman.

When Harry was nine, he and Vivian caught diphtheria. He later wrote, "They gave us ipecac and whiskey. I've hated the smell of both ever since. . . . I was paralyzed for six months after the throat disease left me, and my mother wheeled me around in a baby buggy." He also had a difficult time because of poor eyesight; forced to wear glasses from the age of six, he did not actively participate in sports or roughhouse games, though he was often called upon to clarify rules or mediate disputes among his

Harry, four years old, standing with his younger brother, John Vivian. At the time Harry and his family were living on his grandfather's farm in Grandview, Missouri. In his memoirs Truman wrote of the joyous years he spent there as a child.

neighborhood friends. He was a passionate reader, particularly of history and biographies, and loved the works of William Shakespeare, Charles Dickens, Victor Hugo, and others. Truman said that by the age of 12 he had read everything Mark Twain had published to that point as well as every book in the Independence public library. He also greatly enjoyed playing the piano and often traveled to Kansas City for piano lessons as he grew older.

After high school he hoped to attend the U.S. Military Academy at West Point, New York. He and another boy received special tutoring in history and geography, but Truman failed the required eye exam

At age 10 Truman was already a passionate reader who devoured biographies of great historical figures such as Charlemagne, Napoleon, and Benjamin Franklin. As a young man he applied the lessons he learned from his reading and developed a plan to achieve "greatness."

for both the army and the navy. He attended local business college the summer after high school graduation in 1901 but was prevented from continuing with his education when poor investments led to the collapse of the family finances. He took a job as a timekeeper for a railroad construction company and put some of his clerical training to use. The workmen were mostly hoboes and Truman signed their paychecks in a saloon. They would drink up their wages over the weekend and then show up for work on Monday in order to get fed. Truman later said that the men he worked with "taught me many, many things that had been a closed book to me up to this time," and that he "received a very down-to-earth education in the handling of men" from them.

In 1903 the family left Independence to live in Kansas City, and Harry took a job as a bank clerk there. When the Trumans moved to a farm in Clinton, in southern Missouri, Harry moved into a boardinghouse where several other young bank employees stayed. One of his fellow boarders was Arthur Eisenhower, brother of Dwight Eisenhower, the future World War II hero and Truman's successor as president. He did well as a clerk, achieving a salary of $100 a month in 1905, but an even brighter achievement for Truman in that year was joining the new National Guard unit in Kansas City. Though his eyesight was no better, the unit needed recruits. He enjoyed his blue uniform, the weekly drills, new friendships, and the summer training.

In 1906 he joined his family on a farm near Grandview that had belonged to his maternal grandfather. He later wrote, "I became a real farmer, plowed,

Truman's high-school graduating class in Independence, Missouri, in 1901. He is at top, fourth from the left. Elizabeth Wallace, who married Truman in 1919, is in the second row from the bottom, second from left. At the far left in the front row is Charles Ross, who served as Truman's presidential press secretary.

As a young man Truman believed that those who had achieved greatness had experience in farming, finance, or the military, and he resolved to learn all three. He joined the Kansas City unit of the National Guard in 1905 but left in 1911 to help run the family farm.

sowed, reaped, milked cows, fed hogs, doctored horses, baled hay and did everything there was to do on a 600-acre farm with my father and brother." Truman's reading had convinced him that the great leaders of history had learned finance, farming, and the military, so he pursued this next course of his education with enthusiasm. He read widely in agricultural journals and reports and experimented with his crops. He was the first farmer in Grandview to use crop rotation regularly. His success as a farmer helped make him a community leader. He joined the local Farm Bureau in 1913 and was elected president of the township unit of the bureau the following year. He stayed on the farm until 1917,

Truman in 1908, two years after he had rejoined his family on the farm in Grandview. It was while working on the farm that Truman first became involved in politics, as a member of the Farm Bureau, postmaster, county road overseer, and school-board member.

when he was 33 years old. "It was a great experience. Wish I'd kept a diary," he wrote.

Truman was not all ambition. He liked people and was himself well liked. He once wrote to a friend about a time when he was helping to dig a grave. "It is not nearly such a sad proceeding as you'd think. There were six or seven of us, and we'd take turns at digging. Those who weren't digging would . . . tell lies about the holes they'd dug and the hogs they'd raised. We spent a very pleasant forenoon and then went to the funeral."

Truman got to know his neighbors by joining civic and social groups in Grandview — notably the local chapter of the Freemasons and the Baptist church. Freemasonry, a secret fraternal order with traditionally liberal and democratic views, was a stronghold of midwestern community politics in Truman's day. Men sought admission not to discuss or shape politics as such but to socialize with community leaders. Freemason membership was a mark of acceptance and social merit and important for good standing in the community. As for religion, Truman called himself a "Lightfoot Baptist" — he liked the church except for its disapproval of theater, dancing, and parties. He also took part in local Democratic party politics, receiving appointments as Grandview postmaster, county road overseer, and member of the local school board.

Successful and popular though they were in the community, the Trumans could never get ahead of their debts. This was partly due to John Truman's rule of paying off debts whole, as soon as possible, instead of paying creditors in installments. Harry wrote somewhat despondently to Elizabeth (called "Bess") Wallace, his childhood sweetheart, "I guess you are lucky that you don't care [for me] — as even the best of fellows, which I am not, couldn't very well make a girl happy on nothing a week and a hatfull of debts. You see, I was fool enough or good enough, whichever way you look at it, to go in with daddy even on his debts."

Truman had first met Bess shortly after his family moved to Independence in 1890. "I met a very beau-

Truman carried this photograph of Bess Wallace with him while serving in France during World War I. They were married in 1919, shortly after his return to Missouri.

tiful little lady with lovely blue eyes and the prettiest golden curls I've ever seen. We went through Sunday school, grade school, high school and we're still going along hand in hand," he later wrote in his autobiography. They met when he was six and she was five. Friends while in high school, they corresponded and sometimes visited each other after the Trumans moved away from Independence. They began to court in 1910, got engaged three years later, but did not marry until 1919.

Bess's maternal grandfather, George P. Gates, was the co-owner of a large flour company. One of the most prosperous citizens in Independence, he lived in a large house near the Truman residence. His daughter, Madge, had married David Willock

Most of the European nations had been at war for nearly three years when the United States entered World War I in 1917. Truman arrived in France in early 1918 and soon after was put in command of Battery Company D.

Wallace, a handsome man and a rising politician. Their daughter, Bess, was attractive, athletic, and well-to-do — quite a catch for the struggling, plain-looking Truman. A few years after Bess graduated from high school, David Wallace shot himself with a pistol, abruptly ending his own life and shattering the lives of those who loved him. Years later Bess's daughter would write that Bess never recovered emotionally from her father's suicide and could never again express her love easily to another person.

John Truman had died in November 1914. The long years of trying to earn a living from farming while laboring under the family's debts had worn down Harry's love of the land. Moreover, he needed to make more money if he was to marry Bess (he had been unable to afford an engagement ring), who hated farm life and was eager for him to move on to something else. Disenchanted with farming, in 1916 Truman tried a number of speculative business ventures involving zinc and oil. During that year he wrote constantly to Bess about his hopes of improving his finances. "I seem to have a grand and admirable ability for calling tails when heads come up. My luck should surely change. Sometime I should win. I have tried to stick. Worked, really did, like thunder for ten years to get that old farm in line for some big production. Have it in shape and have had a crop failure every year." His year of speculation ended with few profits.

Truman had little interest in further investments. Farming and finance may have lost their luster, but Truman had never lost his enthusiasm for the military. He had finished his term with the National Guard in 1911 but had reluctantly not rejoined because of his responsibilities in running the farm. In April 1917 President Woodrow Wilson, angered by repeated German submarine attacks on U.S. shipping, announced that the United States would enter World War I on the side of the Allies (France, Great Britain, and Russia) against the Central Powers (Germany, Austria-Hungary, and the Ottoman Empire). The war had begun in 1914 — brought about by political, commercial, and colonial rivalries among the European powers — and had been fought on battlefields in Europe, Asia Minor, and the Middle East. With the overthrow of Russia's autocratic Tsar Nicholas II in March 1917, it was possible to see the war as a struggle between the enlightened, essentially democratic governments of the Allies and the outdated, repressive hereditary monarchies of the Central Powers. "The world must be made safe for democracy," Wilson proclaimed in his war message to Congress on April 2, and Truman reacted enthusiastically to the president's address.

Truman set to work and organized an artillery regiment in Kansas City that was mustered into the Missouri National Guard and then the U.S. Army. He enlisted in June and was elected a first lieutenant by the men of the regiment, having managed somehow to bypass the vision requirement. Many of the men in the regiment were known to Truman from business and his previous National Guard experience. When the unit was sent to Oklahoma for training, it was the first time in Truman's life that he had been away from western Missouri for any length of time.

> *I learned from it that a leader is a man who has the ability to get other people to do what they don't want to do, and like it.*
> —HARRY S. TRUMAN
> on history

While training in Oklahoma Truman also managed the regiment canteen. To the ill-equipped men of the regiment, the well-stocked canteen was something of a godsend, and it greatly boosted the morale of the former National Guardsmen, who were often looked down upon by the regular army soldiers. Truman and Bess had gotten engaged by now, and she sent him a picture of herself to carry with him to the war. By February he was up for promotion to captain, and he was sent in advance of his regiment to France. On the way he stopped in New York City and was typically unimpressed. "New York is a very much over-rated burg. . . . There isn't a town west of the Mississippi that can't show a better time," he wrote Bess.

In France, Truman, now a captain, received advanced artillery training. He learned rapidly, became an instructor, and was soon asked to command Battery Company D. Though the company was somewhat notorious for its lack of discipline and toughness on commanding officers, Truman was able to gain the respect of his men and turn the company into a highly efficient unit.

In August Truman went into combat for the first time. Though he wrote Bess that "my greatest satisfaction is that my legs didn't succeed in carrying me away," his men were impressed by his level-headedness under fire. "You'd have thought that he was sitting in the kitchen of his home with his feet on a chair and about as much worried," one of them wrote. His composure and self-assurance were in evidence throughout the remainder of the war, particularly at the Battle of Argonne Forest in September 1918, where Truman and Battery Company D distinguished themselves. The armistice ending the war came shortly thereafter, in November, and by May 1919 he was back in Kansas City.

Although his time in combat had been brief, his service in the military was an invaluable experience for Truman. His achievements as an officer and as the commander of a group of rowdy, hardened soldiers were a great confidence builder and marked his first unqualified success in any of his chosen fields to that point. He also made extremely important contacts and connections that were to serve him well in his political career. So crucial were these wartime connections that he later said "My whole political career is based upon my war service and war associates."

Success in the military did not immediately translate itself into success in civilian life. After being discharged from the army in May 1919, Truman married Bess and moved into his mother-in-law's large house in Independence. He and a veteran friend, Eddie Jacobson, who had comanaged the regiment canteen, opened a men's clothing store in Kansas City. At first they did well, but then the national economy slipped into a recession and the haberdashery had to close in 1922. At the beginning of their financial troubles in early 1921, Truman and Jacobson had changed the business from a partnership to a corporation. They were able to raise more money that way — from both banks and shareholders. Unfortunately, they were still personally liable for debts undertaken before incorporation. Store merchandise had served as collateral in 1919 and 1920 but by 1922 had lost much of its original value because of decreased consumer demand. Truman later said that his losses totaled $28,000. His

The men of Battery Company D (Truman is at front center) were known for drunkenness and lack of discipline, but under Truman's command they performed admirably, particularly at the Battle of Argonne Forest.

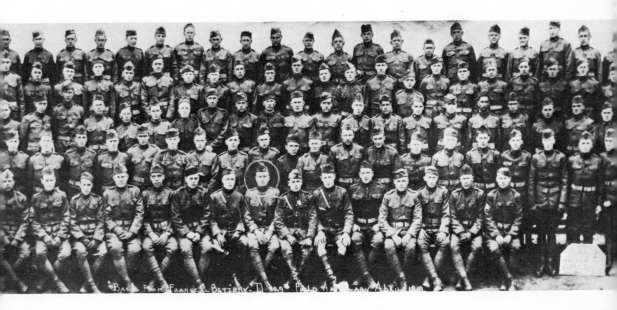

Truman (wearing bow tie) on a picnic with family and friends in Kansas City in June 1921. At the time Truman owned a clothing store that was in serious financial straits.

partner declared bankruptcy, and Truman struggled for 15 years to repay the debts. Later, his political opponents would claim that his business failure proved Truman's lack of ability, but national economic conditions had undermined Truman's chances for success in the clothing business.

At age 38, Truman was still to find his life's work. He decided to try politics. In the army he had met James M. Pendergast, the son of Michael J. Pendergast, who was the older brother of Thomas J. Pendergast, one of a small number of "political bosses" — as the heads of political organizations that could deliver large blocs of votes were called — in Missouri. Patronage jobs, favors for special interests, votes, and campaign contributions were the mediums of exchange used by the political organizations, or "machines." In 1922 Mike Pendergast asked Truman to run as the Democratic party candidate for eastern judge of Jackson County. The Pendergast choice for western judge of the county was a man with unquestioning loyalty to the faction, Henry McElroy.

Truman was a poor speaker at a time when campaign oratory was as decisive as the use of television is in today's elections. To make matters worse, the Pendergast faction all but withdrew its support, concentrating instead on the candidate and district that would give them the most power. Truman used his extensive network of Missouri relatives and war veterans to win the vote. To Pendergast's chagrin, McElroy lost and Truman narrowly won, leaving him with little obligation to the faction. His position was essentially that of a county administrator, not, despite the title, in any sense a judicial or legal officer. The eastern half of Jackson County was rural. (Kansas City was located in the western section.) Truman was responsible for county finances, the budget, and road building. While serving as eastern judge, Truman attended law school at night. He quit school after two years, tired of having to conduct county business at night with those who sought him out in school and even in the library. Even without the degree, the legal training he received proved invaluable later on. Truman was defeated in his quest for reelection in 1924 in the face of powerful opposition from an alliance among the Republicans, two family factions, and the Ku Klux Klan. It was the only election that he ever lost.

Two years after his defeat Truman went to Tom Pendergast and asked for a new job. Pendergast offered him the chance to run for presiding judge of the whole county. The Pendergast faction had increased its power substantially during the time Truman was out of office. Tom Pendergast had allied himself with a rival faction controlled by the Shannon family. Their cooperation ensured that candidates they both endorsed would always win county elections. Also in the Pendergasts' favor was that Kansas City had abolished the office of mayor in favor of a nine-member city council that hired a city manager. A simple majority on the council took the power out of voters' hands and gave it to Pendergast and Shannon. Control of Kansas City and their ability to deliver votes gave birth to the Pendergast machine that ruled Missouri politics for decades. Truman accepted the nomination and won the election easily, serving for eight years in the position.

The political machine of Thomas J. Pendergast (pictured with his wife) used its control of political patronage positions to deliver large blocs of votes and influence municipal, county, and state politics in Missouri. Truman's association with the Pendergast organization began with his campaign for county judge in 1924.

He built roads and a courthouse, administered public-works projects when the Great Depression struck in the 1930s, and created a six-county regional plan that became a model for planners nationwide. Soon he attracted attention as an honest, efficient administrator who was friendly with the Pendergast machine but who was not himself corrupt. According to his daughter, he hoped to go to Congress, but Pendergast did not support his ambitions. In 1932 some supporters started a "Truman for Governor" movement, and Truman tried to convince Pendergast of his statewide support, but Pendergast backed another choice as his candidate.

A Republican senator was up for reelection in 1934. Pendergast's first choices for the office, Joseph Shannon and the Democratic state chairman, Jim Aylward, had turned down the nomination, and Pendergast needed a candidate. The depression and the popularity of the new Democratic president, Franklin Roosevelt, made 1934 a good year for a Democratic candidate. Truman accepted.

The Democratic primary campaign was nasty. Truman's opponents, John Cochran and Tuck Milligan, denounced Truman as the puppet candidate of the Kansas City machine. Rumor had it that Tom Pendergast once boasted that he was sending his "office boy" to the Senate of the United States. Working with a very small amount of money (approximately $9,000), Truman campaigned vigorously and won a narrow primary victory in August, then easily defeated the Republican incumbent in November. Suddenly, at age 51, Harry S. Truman, who was scarcely known by anyone outside of Missouri, was on his way to Washington and the U. S. Senate.

The man who had once written in a journal of his desire to achieve "greatness" of character could now reasonably feel that he had finally achieved some recognition for his efforts in life. He always described himself as a common man, an average man who lacked special abilities and educational background. Indeed, his humility and modesty were often so pronounced that some suspected that he intended to promote the image of a common man because it suited his professional goals.

Clearly, he had a knack for achieving uncommon results if not outright success. He did not make a lot of money in agriculture, but he did become a knowledgeable, modern farmer. He learned scientific methods of breeding livestock and controlling soil erosion as well as modern methods of crop control. As an army officer, he turned an artillery battery with a reputation for being troublesome into a more than capable unit. As the presiding judge of Jackson County, he won a statewide reputation for far-sighted administration. On the surface he appeared ordinary, but his capacity for hard work and his openness, honesty, and personal integrity won the admiration of those who worked with him.

The major question mark on his record involved his relationship with the often corrupt Pendergast machine. A biographer of the young Truman, Richard Lawrence Miller, has written that "Truman played a key role in maintaining the Pendergast control. . . . He not only knew of the machine's illegalities but participated in some of them." The evidence provided in Miller's book demonstrates that Truman was more involved in the activities of the Pendergast organization — which included placing Pendergast cronies on the county payroll and graft in the awarding and execution of state, county, and federal contracts — than once seemed likely. In order to become a successful politician, he became a part of an organization that engaged in corrupt practices.

He certainly did not profit personally from his activities with Pendergast. He once wrote of other members of the machine, "I'm not a partner of any of them, and I'll go out poorer in every way than when I came into office." No one has ever suggested that he took money improperly. He contributed to the machine in other ways: He appointed Pendergast's friends and colleagues to jobs, he approved construction contracts with associates of the machine, and he declared his loyalty to Pendergast on several occasions.

Truman believed that he had no recourse where Missouri politics was concerned. Although Pendergast could not always ensure electoral victories, he

Truman in 1930, during his term as county judge (essentially a county administrator). Historians disagree on the extent of Truman's involvement with the graft and corruption of the Pendergast machine, but most agree that he did not profit personally.

could effectively veto any aspirant to office in western Missouri. Sometimes Truman found himself facing difficult decisions as a consequence of his position. Once he asked in a private note to himself, "Am I an administrator . . .? Or am I just a crook to compromise in order to get the job done? You judge it, I can't."

Over time he discovered that he could usually be his own man and do what he thought best. Indeed, Pendergast may have recognized that there were advantages to supporting a few men who had reputations for integrity. Truman wanted to be an effective leader in government; he prided himself on the results that he achieved for the citizens. This meant in western Missouri that he had to be able to work with Tom Pendergast and his men.

The record indicates that Truman in most instances did what he thought best. He knew that he did not live in a perfect world. The alternative to the Pendergast machine in Missouri was the St. Louis machine, and he preferred to represent the former in the contest for the Senate. He focused on doing an effective job in the environment in which he found himself and did not worry about the greater implications raised by the corruption and graft of the Pendergast machine.

On rare occasions he pointed out the benefits of machine government. In one letter, he complained to a writer, "Your airport, your city hall, your auditorium, your traffic way system, your city-county plan — all are the result of McElroy-Truman-Pendergast vision. Why don't you admit it? You can't of course. . . . No one expects it. But I'm sure history will take care of that." The results, he believed most of the time, justified his efforts.

Throughout his life, Truman defended professional politicians from what he regarded as unfair criticism. He recognized that organization was a necessity in politics. He believed that people raised in privileged circumstances, such as Franklin Roosevelt and Adlai Stevenson, a two-time Democratic presidential candidate in the 1950s, often failed to give credit to the people who made their political successes possible. Moreover, they were likely to know and acknowledge only the very corrupt and inefficient machines, such as New York's Tammany Hall, and therefore misjudge organized politicians in places outside New York City and Chicago.

So Truman maintained his personal honesty while being a loyal supporter of Tom Pendergast's political organization. Pendergast became increasingly involved in illegal activities during the 1930s. Truman voted independently of Pendergast but did not forget him when Pendergast came under fire from law enforcers and was sent to prison for income tax evasion.

Some of Truman's weaknesses as a politician probably resulted from his experience as a member of a political machine. Some people thought that his emphasis on loyalty rather than on ability when making political appointments deprived him of the best knowledge and experience available.

One effect of his involvement with Pendergast was that people in Washington underestimated the new senator from Missouri. He was repeatedly dismissed as a political hack representing Pendergast. This lack of respect may, in some ways, have suited Truman's temperament, for he liked to present himself as the underdog, the common man representing the common people of Missouri in Washington. Soon, however, a few people began to notice the hard work he was doing in the Senate.

Senator Burton K. Wheeler of Montana was one of the first to recognize Truman's potential. He helped the new senator with his work on the appropriations and interstate commerce committees and granted Truman permission to attend Senate hearings investigating railroad finances. Truman was already interested in railroads but became an authority in order to participate in the hearings even though he was not a member of the committee. His performance was impressive, and he was quickly made the vice-chairman. The public responded enthusiastically to his revelations of financial abuses by railroad executives. Truman's hard work in organizing the Civil Aeronautics Board,

A long line of jobless men outside the employment office was a common sight during the Great Depression of the 1930s. Truman, who was elected to the U.S. Senate in 1934, supported the recovery and reform measures proposed by President Franklin Roosevelt to ease the economic devastation.

which regulated the airline industry, also attracted attention and praise.

Supreme Court Justice Louis Brandeis and Chief Justice Harlan Stone, influential progressives on the bench, singled Truman out for discussions about railroad reform legislation. Some of these discussions were then presented to Roosevelt as proposals for legislation. As a result, the Wheeler-Truman Transportation Act was passed in 1940.

Virtually all political activity during the 1930s took place under the long shadow cast by the Great Depression, which began with the collapse of the U.S. stock market in the fall of 1929. As the economy deteriorated in the United States, international financial institutions and markets were affected, in turn having further severe repercussions on American agriculture and virtually all major industries. Unemployment rose from a relatively high figure of 4 million people in 1931 to an astronomical 16 million people — one-third of the work force — in 1932–33. Total national income dropped by more than half, and the wages of those fortunate enough to hang onto jobs in the manufacturing industries

declined by more than 60 percent. More than 100,000 businesses failed; hundreds of banks closed, often taking the life savings of individuals with them. Large numbers of people perished from malnutrition, illness, and related causes, while still more took to the road in an often vain search for work.

Many Americans blamed the depression on the rapacity and greed of those who controlled big business and industry. Roosevelt's election in 1932 may be partially attributed to this feeling. The Republican administration of his predecessor, Herbert Hoover, was seen as indifferent to the sufferings of those hurt by the depression, if not, in its encouragement of big business, responsible for the crash itself. The popular perception of Hoover was of a president paralyzed by the economic crisis, unwilling or unable to propose measures to deal with the matter. Cartoonists portrayed an aloof Hoover dining from fancy china atop fine linen tablecloths in the White House while the newly unemployed prowled the streets looking for food. Shantytowns housing those who had lost their homes sprang up around the country and were called "Hoovervilles."

In contrast, Roosevelt promised to act. In his inaugural address in 1933, he sought to allay the panic of a nation in the midst of an unprecedented calamity, saying that "the only thing we have to fear is fear itself." Based on the theory that government spending could "pump-prime" the depressed economy, Roosevelt proposed a series of relief and recovery measures during his first 100 days in office. Later in his presidency he proposed a further series of acts, designed to achieve substantive social and economic reforms and ensure that nothing on the scale of the Great Depression could ever occur again. Collectively, Roosevelt's programs are known as the New Deal.

Truman's work on the railroad hearings and steadfast support for measures that would aid farming and agriculture stamped him as a populist, as those who opposed big business and supported the interests of agriculture and the so-called little man

> *If he exercises his authority wisely, that is good for the country. If he does not exercise it wisely, that is too bad, but it is better than not exercising it at all.*
> —HARRY S. TRUMAN
> on presidential power

were known. (There had been a Populist party formed to promote agrarian interests in the 1890s.) Consistently stressing the necessity of a healthy agricultural sector for a prosperous national economy, he backed Roosevelt's agricultural measures. Truman was particularly upset by the Supreme Court decision that found the New Deal's Agricultural Adjustment Administration (AAA), which established federal regulation of farm production in order to control market prices, to be unconstitutional.

Truman was a consistent supporter of virtually all the New Deal programs, siding with the president on even his controversial plan to appoint additional Supreme Court justices to achieve a majority favorable to his legislation. Of great importance to his future career was the reputation he gained as a friend of the labor union movement for his support of legislation that would establish a minimum wage and maximum daily working hours.

Despite his support, Truman received little respect from the president, who viewed Pendergast's relationship with the senator in the worst possible light. Roosevelt did not allow Truman any say in federal appointments made in Missouri; to Truman's disgust, all patronage was handled through the senior senator, Bennett Clark, who seemed to

Bess Truman never liked Washington, D.C., preferring life in Independence. Even after she joined her husband in Washington in 1944, their married life was complicated by Bess's mother, Madge Wallace, who lived with them until her death in 1952 and never quite approved of her son-in-law.

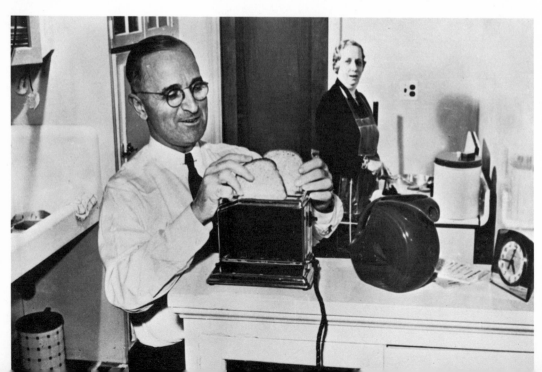

Truman to be lazy and given to excessive drinking. It took Truman five months before he could see the president, and then Roosevelt halted the meeting after only seven minutes. Truman became so upset that he complained publicly to a newspaper, "I'm tired of being pushed around and having the president treat me like an office boy. They better learn downtown right now that no Tom Pendergast or anybody else tells Senator Truman how to vote."

A more important matter kept Truman from fully enjoying his position as senator. His personal life was not complete. In 1924, the Trumans had a daughter, Margaret. Truman was ecstatic about his "Marg," but for most of his first six years in Washington, Bess and Margaret lived in Independence with Bess's mother. Part of the problem was financial: Truman had debts from the collapse of the haberdashery and campaign expenses of the 1934 election, and his salary was not sufficient to pay for a Washington apartment big enough to house Bess, her mother, Margaret, and himself. Compounding the problem was Bess's dislike for Washington. She had friends in Independence, and the acrimony that frequently flared up between her husband and her mother was another argument in favor of the separation.

The Trumans wrote frequent, long letters to each other. His letters reflected his unhappiness. In June 1935 he wrote, "I am getting sick and tired of going out to dinner. I'd like just once to eat a sandwich and go to bed with a clear head." A month later, he added: "We'll never do this again. We've got to work out some way to make ends meet and have a place to live in Washington." The next year he wrote: "I wish you were both here. I am getting cranky and need someone to put me back in a good mood." In 1937, he added, "I just can't stand it without you. If we are poorer than church mice, what difference does it make? There is only one thing on earth that counts with me and that is you and Margie." As 1940 approached, however, the difficulties Truman faced in his campaign for reelection that year threatened to make his disagreements with his wife on where the family should live irrelevant.

3

"The Buck Stops Here"

Once during the 1930s a newsreel crew tried to record on camera one of the rare speeches made by Senator Truman. The crew became increasingly exasperated with his mumbling and bumbling. After several retakes, the cameraman shouted, "Senator, speak up!" When the crew left, Truman heard one man say with disgust, "He ain't no Roosevelt."

Truman was at best average in appearance and height, spoke with a flat, twangy Missouri accent, and wore thick glasses. No one was ever impressed by his appearance or swept off their feet by his personality. He had a good grasp of history but no college degree. Sometimes he felt out of place with the educated elites of Washington. But during his first year in the Senate, where tradition dictated that freshman senators remain silent on the floor, he studied his fellow senators and discovered that several of them were ineffectual. No more than a dozen were leaders. He set his sights on becoming one of the leaders of the Senate, working steadily and systematically in his first term to achieve his goal.

Truman will not make a great, flashy President like Roosevelt. But, by God, he'll make a good President, a sound President. He's got the stuff in him.
—SAM RAYBURN
U.S. congressman, on Truman

Truman was elected to the Senate in 1934. He won the respect of his colleagues through his energy and hard work and was able to use it to great advantage when he faced a tough reelection contest in 1940.

The most difficult obstacle he faced was the need to win reelection to the Senate in 1940. A series of circumstances made victory in the election unlikely. A major problem was the collapse of the Pendergast machine in Kansas City. The influence of the organization had declined due to Tom Pendergast's poor health — he had suffered a heart attack and had undergone an operation for cancer — and legal troubles. He was convicted of tax evasion in 1939 and, though free on parole, was forbidden to participate in politics. Truman could not count on the support of an effective organization in Kansas City, nor could he risk the taint of becoming associated with another political boss. Also troublesome was the decision by Missouri's popular governor, Lloyd Stark, to oppose him in the primary for the Democratic nomination. Stark's popularity was in large part due to his image as the anticrime crusader who had broken the Pendergast machine and other corrupt political organizations. It seemed that Roosevelt initially supported Stark, as he offered Truman the chairmanship of the Senate Interstate Commerce Commission if he would step aside and let Stark have the nomination. Later Roosevelt backed off from supporting Stark, and he never came out publicly for either candidate.

Truman faced long odds. He had not been endorsed by the extremely popular Democratic president. The state's major newspapers, in Kansas City and St. Louis, supported the anticorruption candidate, Stark. Still, Truman's hard work in the Senate paid off. His fellow Senators rallied to the support of their energetic colleague, making speeches and inserting favorable material in the *Congressional Record* that was put to use in election pamphlets. Truman's work on the railroad hearings earned him the backing of the railroad workers, and his reputation as a friend of labor won him the support of labor unions. Veterans and National Guardsmen backed Truman, and he also made use of his track record as a consistent supporter of the New Deal. Although the addition of Maurice Milligan, the state's attorney general whose popularity had risen with the Pendergast prosecutions, seemed a further obstacle for Truman to overcome, it is probable that his candidacy actually cut into Stark's support. Truman won the primary by less than 8,000 votes out of the more than 600,000 cast and was greeted upon his return to Washington with applause from his colleagues. (At the time, Missouri was overwhelmingly Democratic. Winning the primary was tantamount to winning the election.)

An interesting sidelight to Truman's win was the role played by black voters in the election. Although Missouri's black electorate was very small, Truman consciously courted them and credited black votes for his victory. In his private life, there is little doubt Truman was a bigot. He used racial slurs frequently both in conversation and writing, and often repeated racist remarks and jokes. It has been suggested that he actually believed blacks to be inferior to whites. Nevertheless, Truman advocated an end to legal barriers to black opportunity. At the time discrimination against blacks (the so-called Jim Crow laws) was the law in many states. Blacks were discriminated against in education and employment and as a result were far more likely than whites to suffer from poverty. In Missouri, Stark had recently fired all black state workers. Though Truman thought it unlikely that individual race prejudice could be ended — he regarded it as a "misunderstanding" — its institutionalized counterpart was a different matter. He said in a 1940 speech that blacks lagged behind whites in achievement because they were denied educational and other opportunities as a result of legalized discrimination. His opposition to Jim Crow was based on his notions of fundamental decency and the ideals he felt America should stand for. "We owe the Negro legal equality . . . because he is a human being and a natural born American," he said in 1940, and added at another point in the campaign, "In giving the Negroes the rights that are theirs, we are only acting in accord with ideas of true democracy."

Truman began his second term in 1941. As the 1930s drew to a close and the ravages of the depression eased somewhat, American eyes looked outward, toward Europe, where Germany, under the

President Roosevelt received public credit for establishing the War Production Board because of his advance knowledge of this committee's report. That was all right with me. I wanted action more than credit.
—HARRY S. TRUMAN

With the outbreak of World War II in Europe in 1939, military preparedness became the dominant issue in the Senate. Truman gained national attention as the chairman of a committee investigating defense contracts.

Nazi dictator Adolf Hitler, threatened to overrun the continent; and toward Asia, where Japanese military might was building an empire. By signing the Munich Pact with Germany in 1938, France and Great Britain acquiesced to Germany's occupation of the Sudetenland in Czechoslovakia. Recognizing that neither France nor Great Britain was prepared to stand in the way of his territorial ambitions, Hitler removed the other major obstacle to his plans, the Soviet Union, by concluding a mutual non-aggression pact with that nation in August 1939. When Germany invaded Poland the next month, World War II began. Both France and Great Britain declared war on Germany, but neither was militarily prepared to fight. France surrendered to Germany in June 1940.

In the Senate the most pressing immediate question became what steps the United States should take regarding the war. Roosevelt favored a policy of military preparedness and assistance for Great Britain, while in the meantime he gradually edged the nation toward active involvement. Truman essentially supported the Roosevelt policy. Now that he was free of the connection with Pendergast, the New Dealers around Roosevelt seemed to respect him more. As a result, he won approval when he proposed the creation of a special committee to investigate the many defense contracts that were being awarded as the country armed itself. Truman was familiar with the waste, mismanagement, and profiteering that could accompany public contracts through his years of association with the Pendergast organization, and he was determined that the military effort not be undermined by similar corruption. After the United States's entry into the war following the Japanese sneak attack on Pearl Harbor on December 7, 1941, Truman continued his work, lobbying the administration to include small businesses in the awarding of defense contracts and railing against war profiteering and mismanage-

Nominated for the vice-presidency in 1944, Truman at first resisted accepting the position, later claiming that it was "virtually crammed down my throat."

Truman and Roosevelt following the Democratic convention. During the 11 weeks Truman was vice-president, he met with the president only twice and was not kept informed about the conduct of the war.

ment. Truman won widespread admiration for his leadership of the committee and the rigor of the investigation, acquiring a national reputation for fairness and efficiency.

As Truman's national reputation grew, he began to be mentioned as a possible vice-presidential candidate in the 1944 election. The vice-presidential candidate would be extremely important, as Roosevelt's health had begun to give way. The president had been stricken with polio while younger, and he now suffered from a severe heart condition and high blood pressure. Roosevelt's advisers realized that he might not live much longer. The new vice-president might very well become the next president.

John Nance Garner of Texas had been vice-president during Roosevelt's first two terms, but he had retired in 1940. Roosevelt chose Henry Wallace as his successor. Wallace had been Roosevelt's effective, liberal secretary of agriculture. Democratic leaders, however, had become disappointed in him. Though smart and practical, Wallace seemed unstable and injudicious, too liberal, a poor choice for president. The Democratic party regulars felt that Wallace, having never run for office, had a poor grasp of the necessities of electoral politics and told Roosevelt that Wallace would lose voters for the ticket. Roosevelt agreed to consider other candidates for the vice-presidency, and he at least pretended that the decision would be made by others in the party.

Throughout 1944 at least eight different men were considered with some seriousness. Truman was one of those. Interestingly, he was not attracted to the idea. He wrote his daughter, "1600 Pennsylvania [the White House] is a nice address, but I'd rather not move in through the back door — or any other door at sixty."

U.S. troops liberating Paris from the Germans in August 1944, just eight months before the death of Roosevelt. Germany surrendered on May 7, 1945, three weeks after Truman took office, but he still faced complicated questions regarding the occupation of Germany, war reparations, and governments for Eastern Europe.

Roosevelt's funeral procession in April 1945. Roosevelt had been president since 1933 and had led the nation through the depression and World War II. To many, including Truman, his death was as if "the world had come to an end."

Roosevelt's maneuvering further confused the issue. Once, when questioned, he said that although he would not tell delegates to the party convention in Chicago whom they should vote for, he would vote for Wallace. At another time, Roosevelt said that he preferred U.S. Supreme Court Justice William O. Douglas. Just before the convention, Director of War Mobilization James Byrnes, a third candidate, claimed that Roosevelt had endorsed him. Byrnes wanted Truman to formally nominate him at the convention.

Truman had important political appeal from the beginning. He had earned a considerable reputation in the Senate. As the favorite son of a border state, he could command southern electoral votes in a close race. Professional and machine politicians from large cities also favored him, believing that he was one of them. Labor union leaders expressed complete confidence in Truman, and the railway workers were particularly loyal boosters. The chairman of the Democratic National Committee, Robert E. Hannegan, was also in Truman's camp. Hannegan was the former head of the St. Louis machine and had supported Truman in the 1940 Senate campaign.

Truman resisted the nomination. His own health was poor, and his hard work during the war years had left him exhausted. At age 60 he was unsure that he possessed the energy and physical stamina that would be required should he become president. He was also convinced that he could be of greater service to his country as a senator than as vice-president. Years later he wrote in his diary, "Well this job was virtually crammed down my throat in Chicago." Even after arriving in Chicago, he continued to protest against his selection until he heard Hannegan talking to Roosevelt on the telephone.

Truman heard Hannegan say to the president, "He's the contrariest Missouri mule I've ever dealt with." Hannegan held the phone out so that Truman could hear Roosevelt's response, "Tell him that if he wants to break up the Democratic party in the middle of the war, that is his responsibility." Truman's response was, "Well, if that is the situation I'll have to say yes, but why the hell didn't he tell me in the first place." After his acceptance speech, he and Bess fought their way through the crowds at the convention hall. Bess asked quietly, "Are we

Truman was sworn in as president on April 13, 1945. The next day he told some reporters that when he learned Roosevelt had died, "I felt like the moon, the stars, and all the planets had fallen on me."

Japanese *kamikaze* pilots intentionally crashed their planes into U.S. ships during World War II. Such fanatical tactics contributed to the belief that the Japanese would desperately resist an invasion and led Truman to believe that American lives would be saved by dropping the atomic bomb.

going to have to go through this for all the rest of our lives?"

Roosevelt and Truman defeated the Republicans in 1944. Truman did very little during the 11 weeks he was vice-president. Though inactivity and insignificance have usually been the fate of vice-presidents (Truman liked to ask reporters if they could remember the names of past vice-presidents), he was even more neglected than most. The country was at war, yet the second-in-command knew little of the conflict's progress or strategy. He was not told about the Manhattan Project. He did not meet with the secretary of state, Edward R. Stettinius, Jr. Truman later said that he met only twice with Roosevelt during the 11 weeks.

On the afternoon of April 12, 1945, Truman left the Senate chamber. He planned to stop for a drink of bourbon in the office of the speaker of the House of Representatives. Told that the White House press secretary had just summoned him by telephone, he quickly ordered a car and rode down Pennsylvania Avenue. At the White House he was escorted to a study on the second floor. The president's wife, Eleanor, said softly, "Harry, the president is dead." Roosevelt had suffered a massive cerebral hemorrhage. Truman, shocked, asked, "Is there anything I can do for you?" Eleanor Roosevelt replied, "Is there anything we can do for you? For you are the one in trouble now."

He was in trouble. He was following a man who had been president longer than any other. Many people simply could not remember another president. Truman later wrote of traveling on the funeral train with Roosevelt's body: "Every place we stopped there'd be a crowd just as if . . . well, you'd think the world had come to an end, and I thought so, too." Five months later, he wrote Mrs. Roosevelt, "I never think of anyone as the President but Mr. Roosevelt."

In June 1945 the U.S. Marines captured Okinawa and the surrounding Japanese islands. The fall of Okinawa was viewed as the final step before the planned U.S. invasion of the Japanese home islands.

Once he took office, Truman declared his intentions to follow Roosevelt's policies. Differing situations and personalities, however, resulted in numerous policy changes under the new administration.

He announced immediately that he intended to follow Roosevelt's policies. He liked to point to FDR's portrait on the wall and say, "I'm trying to do what he would like." Of course, he could do that only in the most general of ways, because new problems and opportunities emerged soon after Truman became president, and he was a very different person from Roosevelt.

The Truman style differed greatly from Roosevelt's. Roosevelt had come from a wealthy, socially prominent New York family. He received an Ivy League education and was given to a somewhat grand, patrician style. Many of his advisers were from similar backgrounds, and their manner irritated Truman. With his small-town, middle-American background and common-sense, no-nonsense approach, Truman regarded many of the New Dealers as pretentious. He resented their doctrinaire liberalism and intended to pursue the New Deal goals he valued in his own pragmatic, surefooted way. He preferred the term *forward-looking* to *liberal*. "The American people have been through a lot of experiments and they want a rest from experiments," he confided to Clark Clifford.

The White House staff he assembled were almost exclusively Missourians. Some had only their loyalty to Truman to commend them, but some of them were people of real ability. Clark Clifford came to the White House as assistant to Truman's military aide, James K. Vardaman, Jr. Within a year the young attorney had emerged as an excellent adviser.

Truman faced numerous problems. Only George Washington, Abraham Lincoln, and Franklin Roosevelt had faced more difficult problems at the beginning of their terms in office. Truman had to oversee the conclusion of World War II in Europe, develop a strategy to conclude the defeat of Japan, negotiate agreements with the major allies (Great Britain and the Soviet Union) that could serve as a basis for a peaceful future, direct the conversion of the American economy from a wartime to a peacetime economy, and provide leadership for a great nation that now possessed unprecedented power and responsibility in the world.

Perhaps naturally, public attention and curiosity focused on the new president and his family. Overnight the American people had for president a man they knew nothing about. Modest and plainspoken, the Trumans were not natural celebrities and rose to the occasion as best they could. A month after he became president, Truman wrote a friend in Independence: "It is a peculiar American complex to want to know what their president eats, how he sleeps, when he gets up, what meats he prefers, etc. . . ."

Bess was the one most likely to be overlooked. She did her duty graciously, but she still did not like Washington or the publicity of official life. The short, plump, gray-haired wife of the president often went unrecognized even in the capital. Inevitably, she was compared unfavorably with the forceful,

Truman with Bess (right) and their daughter, Margaret. The new president's down-to-earth, simple manner differed greatly from Roosevelt's patrician style.

Truman addressing a joint session of Congress. Despite his seemingly mild manner, the new president acted decisively to take control of his administration. He delegated more authority to his advisers than Roosevelt had and believed that he took a more pragmatic, less doctrinaire approach.

active Eleanor Roosevelt, who had served as her husband's "goodwill ambassador." It seemed symbolic that once when she christened an airplane, she could not crack the champagne bottle even after nine tries.

But it was Truman who attracted the most attention and who now occupied the spotlight. His personality seemed largely unaffected by his new position. He continued to talk, dress, and act in the same simple manner as before. He played the piano, took walks, and sometimes played poker and drank bourbon with his cronies. Occasionally, he would be angered by some comment on the radio or in a newspaper and write an angry, intemperate letter to the offender.

His most immediate goal was to gain control of his own administration. He began by removing most of Roosevelt's cabinet leaders. Within eight months, he had replaced all but two. Knowing the

importance of a good relationship between Congress and the president, he appointed several congressmen to the new cabinet. Truman knew that he would have to depend on his cabinet and advisers for much of his on-the-job training, and he wished to have men he knew and trusted in these positions.

His newness to the position and lack of information on the intricacies of Roosevelt's war strategy precluded Truman from veering significantly from his predecessor's policies in that regard. In leading the United States through the final months of the war, Truman acted as he believed Roosevelt would have, most clearly demonstrated by his concurrence with Roosevelt's insistence on unconditional surrender from Japan and decision to use atomic weapons when Japan failed to comply.

Yet Truman's management style was his own. He met weekly with the entire cabinet, something that Roosevelt had rarely done, if ever. He believed that

Within his first eight months in office, Truman replaced all but two members of the cabinet he inherited from Roosevelt. Pictured are Truman and his cabinet in January 1949. To the right of Truman is Vice-president Alben Barkley.

After two atomic blasts, Emperor Hirohito convinced his military leaders to surrender. On August 14, 1945, the allies accepted the unconditional surrender of the Japanese aboard the USS *Missouri*.

Roosevelt had concentrated too much power in his own hands. Truman sought to delegate greater authority to his subordinates, but he recognized that as president he bore the ultimate responsibility. A sign on his desk that read The Buck Stops Here expressed his conception of the duties of his office. Once he settled into his job, its pressures did not faze him. He often used a homespun aphorism when asked about the burden of the presidency. "If you can't stand the heat," he said, "stay out of the kitchen."

U.S. sailors celebrate the end of World War II. The peace brought with it complex problems for Truman to handle: the reconstruction of the national and international economy, the breakdown of the wartime relationship among the Allies, and the responsibilities the United States now faced as an active participant in global affairs.

4

The Cold War

The most important challenge of Harry Truman's presidency stemmed from the strained relationship between the United States and the Soviet Union. While Americans in 1945 celebrated the victory of the Allies (the United States, Great Britain, the Soviet Union, and France) in World War II, the relationship between the United States and the Soviet Union was deteriorating. By 1946 the conflict was so severe that the term *cold war* began to be used to describe the tense relationship.

Throughout the war, many had hoped that the wartime alliance between the two nations would continue after Germany was defeated and would serve as the basis of an enduring peace. President Roosevelt recognized that continuation of the alliance would be difficult, but he worked at a number of conferences to iron out the problems between the U.S. and Soviet governments. Particularly significant was a February meeting at Yalta in the Soviet Union between Roosevelt, Stalin, and Churchill.

A central concern at Yalta was the future of Poland. Britain had entered World War II when Germany attacked Poland; Churchill and Roosevelt

> *Force is the only thing the Russians understand.*
> —HARRY S. TRUMAN

On the eve of his 62nd birthday, in May 1946, Truman smiles for the camera. At the time, however, his administration was faced with a breakdown in its relations with the Soviets. The cold war between the United States and the Soviet Union dominated American foreign policy in the postwar period.

wanted to be certain that Poland was a free country after the war. The Soviet Union had a considerable interest in seeing that a government friendly to its interests was installed. The Germans had twice in the 20th century launched invasions of the Soviet Union from Poland. Combined Soviet casualties from the two wars numbered in the tens of millions. Clearly, the Soviets had a right to protect themselves from future attacks. Roosevelt and Churchill, fearing that the Soviet security interests would lead the Soviets to force a communist government on a populace unable to resist, sought a representative, democratically elected government.

Similarly complicated was the question of postwar Germany. The Soviet Union had suffered the greatest wartime losses of any of the Allied powers. Stalin spoke of dividing Germany into several states and wanted to collect heavy reparations, in the form of money and goods, from Germany. Mindful that it was the heavy reparations forced on a defeated Germany by the Allies after World War I that contributed greatly to the rise of Hitler, Churchill and Roosevelt hoped to persuade the Soviets to accept less punitive reparations.

Partial agreements, often ambiguously worded, were reached at Yalta. The Soviets, because their armies already occupied Poland, had organized a communist government there, but Stalin promised to admit a few democratic leaders and hold free elections as soon as possible after the war ended. Stalin would also establish interim governments "broadly representative of all democratic elements" in Austria, Hungary, Czechoslovakia, Bulgaria, and Romania with free elections to follow. The Soviets would be allowed to collect some reparations from Germany, but the final decisions on boundaries and the future shape of the German economy would be made later. Moreover, the Soviet Union moderated some of its policies on the issue of an international organization, making possible the creation of the United Nations (UN) after the war ended. Finally, Stalin agreed to become an ally in the attack on Japan after Germany was defeated, in return for which he received territorial concessions in the Far East. With the success of the Manhattan Project still uncertain, Soviet participation in the Asian theater of the war was extremely important to Roosevelt. The Soviet agreement on that point and the United Nations points made the conference a success in Roosevelt's eyes.

Churchill and Roosevelt were soon protesting that Stalin had not kept his word on Poland. Truman, when he became president, had to face the problems presented by the Soviet refusal to hold elections in Poland and by the inability of the two countries to agree on Germany.

Less than two weeks after taking office, Truman met with the Soviet Union's foreign minister, Vyacheslav Molotov, to discuss some of these problems. The meeting took place in the White House and had been arranged so that the Americans and the Soviets could attempt to settle some of their differences prior to the conference for the establishment of the UN. Truman was advised by W. Averell Harriman, U.S. ambassador to the Soviet Union, and Charles Bohlen, a Soviet expert in the State Department, to take a strong position in his meeting with Molotov.

When Truman met with the Soviet ambassador, he said firmly that Stalin should keep his word as given at Yalta. Molotov protested that Poland was an issue for the Soviet Union to settle. Truman insisted that the Soviets must abide by the Yalta agreements. As the meeting ended, Molotov protested, "I've never been talked to like that in my life." Truman snapped back, "Carry out our agreements and you won't get talked to like that." Bohlen, who was the translator at the meeting, later wrote, "How I enjoyed translating those words. They were probably the first sharp words uttered during the war by an American president to a high Soviet official." Over the next two years, sharp words increased in number, and the disagreements between the two nations increased.

Truman tried direct personal negotiation with Stalin at Potsdam but the two were not able to concur on Poland and governments for the rest of East-

He takes no notice of delicate ground, he just plants his foot down firmly upon it.
—CHURCHILL
on Truman at Potsdam

Secretary of State George C. Marshall developed the Marshall Plan to stimulate European economic recovery after the war. In 1953 he received the Nobel Peace Prize for his work.

ern Europe. In June 1946 the U.S. representative to the UN Atomic Energy Commission, New York businessman Bernard Baruch, presented a plan for international control of atomic energy. The Soviets protested the plans for UN control of raw materials needed for atomic energy, operation of plants that processed materials for weapons, direct research, licensing of nuclear activities, and the provisions for punishment of nations that violated the agreement. The Soviets felt the measures needlessly hampered national sovereignty. As their own work on developing an atomic bomb was progressing, acceptance of the Baruch plan would effectively mean that the Soviets could not build their own bomb. Debate among the members of the commission went on for months and was finally left unresolved. Two months later the Soviet Union proposed joint Soviet-Turkish defense of the Dardanelles and the Bosporus, two straits that together linked the Black Sea to the Mediterranean. In response, Truman dispatched a U.S. naval task force to the Mediterranean and relayed through diplomatic channels the opinion that Turkey should continue as the only country responsible for the defense of the straits. Tensions between the two nations increased.

In early 1947 Truman made a critical decision. He was aided by his new secretary of state, George C. Marshall, who had been army chief of staff during World War II. In February the two men confronted a series of crises. Communist parties in France and Italy had made great gains. Britain was close to bankruptcy, and the Soviet Union threatened to control all of Eastern Europe. On February 21, Great Britain informed the president that the British would no longer be able to provide military aid to Greece and Turkey; if the United States thought such aid important, then it would have to provide the funds and material.

Truman and Marshall thought that the United States must help Greece and Turkey to stand firm against possible communist encroachment. The situation was regarded as particularly grave in Greece, where Communist guerrillas were engaging in a civil war. U.S. representatives believed the Soviet Union viewed Greece as a "ripe plum ready to fall into their hands."

In a meeting with congressional leaders, Under Secretary of State Dean Acheson described the reasoning of the administration in graphic language. He recalled his words in a memoir published later: "Like apples in a barrel infected by one rotten one, the corruption of Greece would infect Iran and all to the east. . . . The Soviet Union was playing one of the greatest gambles in history at minimal cost. . . . We and we alone were in a position to break up the play."

After listening to Acheson, Republican senator Arthur Vandenberg of Michigan had some advice for Truman. A former isolationist (one who believes a nation should remain uninvolved in foreign affairs), Vandenberg was now convinced that the United States had to take a role in world affairs. The pres-

If Greece was lost, Turkey would become an untenable outpost in a sea of Communism. Similarly, if Turkey yielded to Soviet demands, the position of Greece would be extremely endangered.
—HARRY S. TRUMAN

ident would have to claim that role on the country's behalf. Vandenberg said that he should "make a personal appearance before Congress and scare the hell out of the American people."

On March 12, 1947, Truman announced to Congress the "Truman Doctrine." He asked for $400 million in military aid for Greece and Turkey. More importantly, he promised future help to other nations that might be in danger of communist insurrection: "I believe that it must be the policy of the United States to support free peoples who are resisting attempts of subjugation by armed minorities or by outside pressure."

Truman's words were alarming. Some Americans, such as Walter Lippmann, a prominent American journalist, recognized that the United States did not

In 1947 George Kennan, a State Department adviser, wrote an article in *Foreign Affairs* magazine urging that the United States oppose the Soviet Union's expansionist designs on Western Europe. His theory, called containment, became the cornerstone of Truman's foreign policy.

have the power to support all "free peoples." Decades later, some Americans would conclude that Truman's policy justified military interventions of the kind that led directly to the tragedy of Vietnam.

His address won the support of Congress, and he followed the announcement with two enactments of the policy. First, Secretary of State Marshall announced a program that became known as the "Marshall Plan" — providing American aid (up to $22 billion) over four years to restore European prosperity. The assumption was that prosperity would lead to a decrease in the numbers of Europeans supporting Communist parties as well as benefit the U.S. economy by allowing for greater purchase of U.S. exports. The terms of the aid package, which called for an integrated plan for all of Europe rather than individual nations, was unacceptable to the Soviet Union and its satellite nations of Poland, Czechoslovakia, Yugoslavia, and Romania. Though constructive and badly needed by the ravaged European economy, the Marshall Plan thus also served to hasten the division of Europe into two essentially hostile camps — Western Europe, allied with the United States, and Eastern Europe, allied with the Soviet Union. On April 4, 1949, the United States entered into the North Atlantic Treaty Organization (NATO) agreement, a mutual defense pact among Belgium, Canada, Denmark, France, Great Britain, Iceland, Italy, Luxembourg, the Netherlands, Norway, Portugal, and the United States. For the first time in American history, the United States signed a treaty of alliance during peacetime.

The goal of Truman's policies was "containment," as articulated by George Kennan, the State Department's preeminent expert on the Soviet Union. Kennan believed that the Soviet Union was bent on expanding its power and influence. Kennan recognized that the United States could not act directly against the Soviet Union and could do little about Soviet influence in Eastern Europe, where the Soviets were firmly established, but he argued that it was in the best interests of the United States to contain any further attempts at Soviet expansion.

> *I think the world now realizes that without the Marshall plan it would have been difficult for western Europe to remain free from the tyranny of Communism.*
> —HARRY S. TRUMAN

After World War II Germany and the city of Berlin were divided among the Allies into zones of occupation. When the Soviet Union blockaded West Berlin, Truman organized an airlift of food and supplies to the stranded West Berliners.

The major test of Truman's policies came in Germany in 1948. The Allies had agreed to divide Germany into four zones of occupation following the war. Berlin, the capital, was similarly divided, but it lay within the Soviet zone of occupation. In June 1948 the Soviets cut off access to West Berlin (the U.S., French, and British sector) by blockading the roads and railroads across their zone of occupation (now East Germany). Truman could have allowed West Berlin to become part of the Soviet zone in Germany, or he could have used military force against the Soviet armies; instead, he called for an airlift to provide food and supplies to West Berlin. The Berlin airlift was a dramatic but nonprovocative announcement to the world that the United States was committed to the protection of Western Europe.

Very gradually, economic prosperity returned to France, West Germany, and Britain. European Communist parties had influence but not enough power to lead governments. Soviet expansion in Western Europe was halted, but the breakdown of the wartime alliance left a divided Europe. West Germany emerged as a strong and prosperous ally of the very nations that had so recently defeated her. Churchill said that an "iron curtain" had descended over Europe, behind which hid the Soviet Union and its Eastern European allies.

The limitations of the Truman Doctrine — that the United States was unable to intervene anywhere in the world and direct the course of events — were most revealingly illustrated by events in China, where the civil war that had been fought between the Nationalists under Chiang Kai-shek and the Communists led by Mao Zedong resumed at the end of World War II.

The U.S. policy had been one of support for Chiang, in the hope that he could establish an effective, responsible government in China, but Chiang's government was badly flawed. Americans in China noted widespread inefficiency, brutality, and corruption, and Mao and the Communists gained popular support. Truman and Marshall dismissed the notion of increasing American aid for Chiang, believing it would likely make the situation

Chinese communists, victors in the civil war against Chiang Kai-shek's Nationalists, enter the capital city of Beijing (Peking) in May 1949. Their leader, Mao Zedong, is pictured on the center poster. Truman's administration was extensively criticized for "losing" China to the communists.

worse. Mao was victorious in 1949 and established a government. The Truman administration was heavily criticized in the United States for having "lost" China.

Another extremely complex crisis involved British-controlled Palestine, to which many of the world's Jews had immigrated in the hope of establishing a Jewish state. The issue had taken on greater importance for European Jews in the 1930s and 1940s with the rise to power of Adolf Hitler and the implementation of his "final solution," a plan to exterminate all of the world's Jews. An estimated 6 million Jews were killed by Hitler during the war. American Jews had been pressuring the U.S. government to take up the cause of a Jewish homeland in Palestine. Jews who had already settled in Palestine made similar appeals to the British, while some groups resorted to terrorist tactics against the British. The Arabs who had made Palestine their home naturally opposed plans for a Jewish homeland there.

Truman had supported the idea of a Jewish homeland when he was a senator and continued to do so as president, but he was criticized by American *Zionists* (supporters of the Jewish homeland) who felt that he was not doing enough to support Jewish immigration to Palestine. Truman countered such criticisms by explaining that Palestine was not an American problem as such and that the Arabs in Palestine also had to be considered. Truman also did not want the issue to damage the U.S. relationship with Britain, which was the nation's most important ally, and spent three years trying to get the question settled through the United Nations.

In late 1947 the General Assembly of the United Nations, under strong pressure from the Truman administration, voted in support of partitioning the area into separate Jewish and Arab states. Arab protests against the resolution turned violent, and the question of who would enforce the partition and resolve the armed conflict arose. The British announced that they would turn over Palestine to the UN on May 14, 1948, but that they would not take responsibility for carrying out the plan. In the meantime State Department experts became convinced that the partition was unworkable and that the enmity U.S. support for the partition would earn it in the Arab world was too high a price to pay. Furthermore, the British withdrawal would quite possibly mean that U.S. troops would be called upon to enforce the partition plan. A lack of communication between the State Department and the White House resulted in State Department officials announcing to the UN that the United States no longer supported partitioning Palestine. The turnabout brought a hailstorm of criticism to Truman, who wrote in his diary: "This morning I find that the State Department has reversed my Palestine policy. The first I know about it is what I see in the papers! . . . I am now in the position of a liar and a double-crosser."

Eventually, the Jews themselves seized the initiative and used their own armies (originally formed to harass British rule) to create by force the new state of Israel. The United States quickly recognized the new nation. The affair was not handled with complete success, as armed conflict betwen Arabs and Jews continued through the late 1980s. Truman was criticized by Zionists, Arabs, and British leaders, who chose to interpret Truman's acknowledgment of the intense and unrelenting pressure from Jewish leaders as calculating concern for American Jewish votes in the presidential election of 1948, but the issue of Palestine was so extraordinarily complex that ill will was certain to result from whatever decision he made.

It is difficult to overestimate the significance of Truman's foreign policy. Under his leadership the United States took a more active role in foreign affairs than previously, and his programs established the basic thrust of U.S. foreign policy for the next 40 years.

Although the end of World War II, the reconstruction of Europe, the establishment of a coherent U.S. foreign policy for the postwar world, and other foreign policy crises dominated the bulk of Truman's first three years in office, domestic issues became

> *He rarely philosophized about the future of the world. He preferred to address himself to the practicalities of the questions.*
> CHARLES BOHLEN
> —U.S. diplomat, on Truman at Potsdam

Coal miners and railroad workers struck in April and May of 1948, paralyzing industry and transportation. Truman forced a settlement by threatening to draft striking workers into the military. "If you think I'm going to sit here and let you tie up this country, you're crazy as hell," he told railroad union leaders.

increasingly important as the 1948 presidential election drew near. An early domestic problem had been the food shortage of 1945–6, which some Americans blamed on Truman. More serious was an outbreak of industrial strikes in 1946 and 1947. Part of the problem stemmed from the erratic leadership of John L. Lewis of the United Mine Workers of America. Truman wrote of Lewis: "He is, as all bullies are, as yellow as a hound dog pup." Truman overreacted to the strikes; he ordered government seizures of the coal mines, the railroads, and other industries.

As a result of the problems of his first 18 months in office, the public became increasingly critical. His approval rating in the Gallup Poll declined from 87 percent to only 32 percent approval in November 1946. Anti-Truman jokes became popular: "To err," said Republicans, "is Truman." Not surprisingly, in

1946 the Republicans won tremendous victories in the congressional elections. High inflation and Truman's inability to win congressional approval for social security measures, education bills, a civil rights act, and education and urban renewal measures contributed to the popular image of him as a man overmatched by the responsibilities of his position.

Truman's chances of winning the election of 1948 appeared bleak indeed. He was surrounded by critics. In 1946, he broke with his secretary of commerce, Henry Wallace, whom he had defeated for the vice-presidency in 1944. Wallace accused Truman of repudiating Roosevelt's foreign policy by encouraging anti-Soviet actions. In 1948 Wallace declared himself the presidential candidate of a new Progressive party and entreated all liberal and peace-loving Americans to vote for him for president.

Despite his statements that he would not be a candidate, Democratic party leaders beseeched General Dwight D. Eisenhower (right) to accept the party's nomination for president in 1948. Truman's own candidacy appeared untenable, as he had lost the support of southern Democrats and the party's liberal wing.

Truman was an advocate of civil rights at a time when overt racism was prevalent throughout the United States. The so-called Jim Crow laws maintained racial segregation in many states. Shown here is a Ku Klux Klan rally shortly after Truman's 1948 address to Congress calling for civil rights legislation.

Even more dangerous to Truman's chances was the effort by some prominent Democrats to convince General Dwight D. Eisenhower, the leader of American forces in Europe during World War II, to run against Truman for the Democratic party nomination. Many years later, Eisenhower said that Truman had promised to support him for the nomination in 1948 but then reneged; Truman denied Eisenhower's account. At any rate, Eisenhower refused to campaign for the nomination. Disaffected Democrats tried to find other candidates, but none proved viable. Finally, they had to accept Truman. Signs at the Democratic party convention said, We're Just Mild About Harry.

Truman had presented Congress with civil rights legislation in February 1948. Later in the year Truman imposed executive orders that ended segregation in the armed forces and also outlawed discrimination in the federal civil service. At the Democratic convention in July a strong civil rights plank was added to the party platform. The result was widespread hostility toward Truman in the

South, where racial segregation was deeply rooted. Southern Democrats (popularly called Dixiecrats) broke with the party and nominated Governor Strom Thurmond of South Carolina for the presidency. The unpopular Truman had to run against the Republican nominee, Governor Thomas Dewey of New York, without the support of his party's southern and liberal wings.

Heeding the advice of Clark Clifford, Truman centered his campaign on Congress's performance, not his own. It was the Republican-dominated Congress that was responsible for America's domestic problems. It was Congress, not the president, that had passed the Taft-Hartley Act — which attempted to restrict the collective bargaining rights of unions — and then overridden Truman's veto. It was Congress that had opposed federal aid to education. Congress had not acted to pass farm price supports, and Congress had stymied Truman's civil rights initiative.

Truman and Senator Alben Barkley of Kentucky, the Democratic party's nominees for president and vice-president, shake hands at the 1948 convention. Few thought the Democrats would defeat the strong Republican ticket of Governor Thomas Dewey of New York and Governor Earl Warren of California.

Truman conducted a vigorous whistle-stop campaign in 1948, often addressing crowds from the rear of his railroad car. He blamed the failures of his administration on Congress, calling it the worst in history. Dewey promised efficiency in government, but Truman reminded voters that the efficiency of the last Republican president, Herbert Hoover, had resulted in the Great Depression.

Truman hammered home his message during the campaign, most of which was conducted by train. He traveled 31,700 miles, snaking across America, stopping to make numerous speeches from the platform on the rear of the train. Never effective when reading speeches, he had learned to deliver sharp, forceful talks from a few prepared notes. In Ohio, the Democratic candidate for governor was reluctant at first to travel with Truman, but he soon discovered that Truman was attracting the largest, most enthusiastic crowds he had ever seen in the state.

Dewey, meanwhile, was overconfidently delivering trite, set speeches. "Our streams," he said, "should abound with fish." He promised to "cooperate with the farmer to protect all the people from

the tragedy of another dust bowl." Polling experts found Dewey far ahead and foolishly stopped taking polls in late October. Well into election night, Dewey was still expected to win. Most Americans were astonished to discover the next morning that Truman had been elected. A famous photograph of Truman was taken that morning as he held aloft a copy of the *Chicago Tribune* announcing his defeat.

It was the high point of his years as president. He won 24.1 million to Dewey's 22 million votes. His emphasis on the failures of the Republican-controlled Congress brought a Democratic majority to the Senate and the House. Although he was hurt by Wallace's and Thurmond's candidacies, he survived the challenge, calling upon the New Deal coalition of voters — labor, blacks, and the urban vote — and was now president in his own right.

"Ain't the way I heard it," exclaimed a jubilant Truman as he held up the *Chicago Tribune*'s premature headline announcing his defeat on the morning after his victory. The support of blacks, labor, and urban voters was responsible for Truman's victory.

5

Second Term and Final Years

Presidents often expect their second terms to be easier than their first. Truman had particular cause to believe this would be so. Combined with his own electoral mandate, the Democrats had won in Congress, which promised to make it easier for Truman to get legislation passed. Many presidents, however, experience severe disappointments in the second term. Such was the case for Harry S. Truman.

The term started with a spectacular inauguration. The pre-election House of Representatives had assumed that Dewey would win; to celebrate the Republican return to power after 16 years of Democratic rule they voted a large sum of money for the inaugural celebration. In addition, they doubled the salary of the president from $50,000 to $100,000. Even nature helped. "The weather. . . ," said Margaret Truman, "was perfect, very cold, but with bright winter sunlight pouring down from a clear blue sky."

In the first few months, the NATO agreement was finally signed, and the Berlin airlift was concluded

> *I'm going to fight hard. I'm going to give them hell.*
> —HARRY S. TRUMAN
> during reelection campaign

Truman and Barkley at their inauguration in January 1949. Truman's last years in office were dominated by the Korean War and the anticommunism movement in the United States.

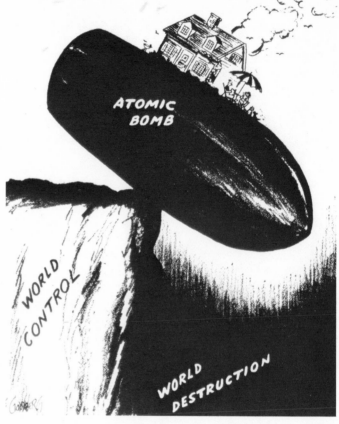

"Peace Today," a 1947 cartoon by Rube Goldberg, depicts American society perched upon the atomic bomb, which offers the potential for world control or world destruction. Truman's September 1949 announcement that the Soviet Union had successfully tested an atom bomb marked the beginning of the arms race between the United States and the Soviet Union.

when the Soviets removed their blockade. In addition, the "Point Four" program was presented to the Congress, resulting in the beginnings of foreign aid to poor third world nations. It was at this time that Truman first used the term that he hoped would sum up his goals in domestic policy — the "Fair Deal."

In September 1949 the United States learned that the Soviet Union had successfully tested an atomic bomb. American experts had known that Soviet scientists would be able to develop a bomb, but they had not expected it to be completed for another four or five years. In January 1950 the United States announced that it would begin work on a new, hydrogen bomb. Truman feared that Soviet scientists might complete such a new bomb ahead of the United States. Two years later, the Americans had the hydrogen bomb; by 1955, the Soviets had one also. The nuclear arms race was under way in earnest.

Meanwhile, Truman's Fair Deal reform bills did not fare well in Congress. He had proposed a series of reforms — national health insurance, increased federal aid to education, a national public housing program, repeal of the Taft-Hartley Act, and a new civil rights bill. Congress passed only the housing program, and it did that solely because it was supported by the Republican leader in the Senate, Robert Taft. Truman wrote in his diary about the new Congress: "Trying to make the 81st Congress perform is and has been worse than cussing the 80th. . . . I've kissed and petted more consarned S.O.B. so-called Democrats and left-wing Republicans than all the presidents and left-wing Republicans put together."

Truman's influence in Congress was even more greatly diminished by the growing anticommunism movement in the United States. Many Americans had been suspicious of communism since Russian Communists had overthrown Tsar Nicholas II in 1917 and established the world's first communist state. Opponents of Roosevelt's New Deal policies denounced the programs as "socialistic" or "communistic," seeing socialist thought at work in their emphasis on an activist role for the federal government in regulating various sectors of the economy, as opposed to strict private ownership of industry with the government playing a hands-off role. (Under socialism, business and industry are owned by the government. Under communist theory, there is no private ownership; industry is owned collectively by the workers.) As American mistrust of the Soviet Union grew with Stalin's initial alliance with Hitler and the revelation of abuses within the Soviet Union such as denial of civil rights and purges of political enemies, so did American antipathy toward communism. The breakdown of the wartime alliance between the Soviet Union and the United States and the onset of the "us against them" mind-set of the cold war period strengthened these feelings. The

The real problem was not how to achieve full employment. It was how to maintain it.
—HARRY S. TRUMAN
on one aim of the Fair Deal

91

The anticommunism campaign of Senator Joseph McCarthy (right, with staff chief Francis Carr) played upon the cold-war fears of many Americans. McCarthy used unfounded allegations and outright lies to create a virtual hysteria about communism. Truman called McCarthyism a threat to every citizen, but it was not until McCarthy attacked the military in 1954 that his power was broken.

accusation that Alger Hiss, a former State Department official, was a former member of the American Communist party and had passed classified material to the Soviet Union, and the discovery of spy rings that had provided the Soviets with atomic secrets, made the Truman administration's "softness" on communism a campaign issue in 1948. Though Truman denounced the issue as a red herring proffered by the Republicans to distract attention from more important questions, politicians seized on anticommunism as a hot issue that gained them favor with the public.

In early February 1950 an obscure senator from Wisconsin, Joseph R. McCarthy, delivered a speech to the Republican Women's Club in Wheeling, West Virginia, in which he said, "While I cannot take time to name all the men in the State Department who have been named as members of the Communist party and members of a spy ring, I have here in my hand a list of 205 that were known to the secretary of state as being members of the Communist party and who nevertheless are still working and shaping the policy of the State Department."

It was the first salvo in what would become more than four years of reckless, largely unfounded accusations made by McCarthy and others. Many individuals within the government, the military, education, the clergy, and entertainment and the arts were accused of being communists. Witnesses before congressional committees were pressured to name other persons suspected of being communists or having "left-wing tendencies." Failure to cooperate often meant a jail sentence. Individuals were blacklisted, or denied employment, because of their suspected political beliefs. Careers and lives were ruined. Within a year the cartoonist Herblock (Herbert Block) coined the term *McCarthyism* to refer to McCarthy's irresponsible tactics.

Although generally without basis, McCarthy's allegations created an atmosphere of suspicion that hurt the Truman administration. Truman had been sensitive to the anticommunism issue for some time. Partly to defuse criticism, in 1947 he had established the Federal Loyalty Program, which investigated the loyalty of federal employees, but charges that the Truman administration was not sufficiently severe against communism continued, growing louder with the victory of Mao and the Communists in China in 1949. Truman's foreign policy was hobbled by charges that the State Department was harboring communists and the strident denunciations of Secretary of State Dean Acheson by McCarthy's backers. Congress was reluctant to pass social welfare legislation, as such measures smacked of New Dealism and socialism. Truman was quick to recognize McCarthy as an irresponsible demagogue but was unable to counter him effectively, and the atmosphere of hysteria that McCarthyism engendered did his administration great harm.

Complicating matters was Korea, where war broke out in 1950. On the evening of June 24 Truman was in Independence, enjoying a vacation from the turmoil of Washington. A telephone call ended any hope of rest. It was Dean Acheson with news

A prisoner of a bunch of twisted intellectuals who tell him what they want him to know.
—SENATOR JOSEPH MCCARTHY
describing Truman

93

Truman made Dean Acheson secretary of state following Marshall's resignation in late 1948. The aristocratic Acheson became the focal point of criticism that the Truman administration was soft on communism, particularly in light of Acheson's support for Alger Hiss, a former State Department official accused of passing classified documents to the Soviet Union.

that communist North Korea had attacked South Korea. Truman considered flying back to Washington immediately, but nighttime air travel was considered very dangerous. He decided to wait until morning and see how serious the crisis was.

At lunchtime on Sunday the 25th, Acheson called again. Nearly 135,000 North Koreans were crossing the 38th parallel, which divided the two countries. The army of South Korea was unable to resist effectively. Truman hurried back to Washington.

Korea was yet another example of a postwar crisis that developed from the breakdown of the U.S.-Soviet wartime alliance. Korea had been under Japanese rule since 1910. Upon Japan's defeat in World War II, the United States and the Soviet Union agreed to divide the country into two sectors, at the 38th parallel, in order to administer the Japanese surrender. When the two nations were unable to agree upon a plan for free elections to reunite Korea, two separate governments and countries were established, each claiming to represent the entire Korean nation.

According to his daughter, Truman at first feared that the North Korean invasion was the "opening round" of World War III. While he soon learned that this was not true, he regarded Korea as a "test" analogous to the 1931 invasion of Manchuria (three provinces in northeast China) by the Japanese. Had Japan been met with firm resistance in 1931 by the great powers of the world, Truman felt, it would have learned that aggression would not work and the Asian portion of World War II might have been avoided. The North Korean invasion was also seen as analogous to German aggression in Europe prior to World War II. As the world's communist states were seen as belonging to one monolithic bloc, controlled by the Soviet Union, it was feared that a passive response in Korea would encourage Soviet expansionism. The recent events in China and McCarthy's accusations also created political pressure on the president to respond to communist provocation.

Apparently Truman decided quickly that the United States should respond with force. On the drive in from the Washington airport on the 25th, he told his advisers, "By God, I am going to hit them hard." Within a week, he and his advisers went to the United Nations to get a cease-fire resolution;

In June 1950 communist North Korea invaded South Korea. Truman immediately committed U.S. troops, technically under the jurisdiction of the United Nations, to resist the North Koreans.

General Douglas MacArthur commanded the UN military forces during the Korean War. His repeated criticism of Truman's conduct of the war led Truman to fire him for insubordination and raised fundamental questions about the principle of civilian control of the military.

then he ordered American warships, planes, and soldiers to rescue South Korea. Officially, the "police action" in Korea was an action of the United Nations, but 90 percent of the soldiers were American.

American troops hurried into South Korea. They were led by General Douglas MacArthur, supreme allied commander in the Pacific during World War II. MacArthur was a strong, publicity-conscious general with a somewhat imperious manner. A biographer later called him an "American Caesar." At the time of the attack on South Korea, his staff feared waking him to tell him of the crisis. Indeed, George Marshall had once told MacArthur, "General, you don't have a staff; you have a court."

Armed with Soviet and Chinese weapons, the North Koreans easily pushed back the South Korean and UN troops, capturing Seoul, the South Korean capital, and much of that country. The troops under

MacArthur helped the South Koreans maintain a hold on the southeast tip of the Korean peninsula. After more troops arrived, General MacArthur led a successful landing at Inchon, near the 38th parallel in South Korea's northwest corner, well behind the advancing North Korean troops. Caught in a pincer movement, the North Koreans scrambled back across the 38th parallel. By October, all enemy troops had been driven from South Korea.

Truman then made one of the most important decisions of his presidency. He could have proclaimed the Korean War a great success. North Korean aggression had been halted, and communism had been contained within its North Korean borders. The war had achieved its original objectives and could have been successfully ended.

Instead, Truman permitted MacArthur to cross the 38th parallel and enter North Korea. Suddenly, the goal shifted from containment of North Korea to its liberation. Public opinion strongly supported rolling back communist power. MacArthur and Acheson, for very different reasons, advised the president to take the offensive and try for a total victory.

Korean refugees during the war. Korea's civilian population suffered greatly during the three-year war (a truce was signed in July 1953). Cities and countryside in both the north and the south were heavily damaged; more than 1 million South Korean civilians were killed and more than 2.5 million were displaced.

As the American armies pushed the North Koreans north to the Yalu River, the boundary between Korea and China, the Chinese issued ominous warnings. Foreign Minister Chou En-lai said that the Chinese would not "supinely tolerate seeing their neighbors being savagely invaded by imperialists." Alarmed, Truman hurried to the Pacific to meet with MacArthur; the general assured him that the Chinese would not intervene and that if they did he would crush them easily.

On November 26, 1950, Chinese divisions suddenly smashed through the center of MacArthur's lines. After a hasty retreat, American forces rallied below the 38th parallel. By the spring of 1951, American and Chinese forces had established a relatively stable front near the 38th parallel. The war became a seesaw struggle across that original boundary; the fighting brought heavy casualties but no territorial gains.

Now MacArthur warned of the "bottomless well of Chinese manpower." He requested permission to bomb China north of the Yalu River; then he called for a naval blockade of China and for the use of Chinese Nationalist troops, now on the island of Taiwan, under Chiang Kai-shek. Truman rejected MacArthur's proposals, for he feared that to attack China would be to force the Soviet Union to come to China's aid.

MacArthur countered by criticizing the president openly to the American news correspondents covering the war. In March 1951 MacArthur issued a public statement that China could be defeated if he were allowed to take the proper steps, which had the immediate effect of sabotaging a proposed cease-fire initiative. In succeeding weeks he made similar statements, even writing to Congressional leaders to complain about U.S. policy. Under the Constitution, the president is the commander in chief of the military. Truman felt MacArthur was insubordinate. His criticisms raised constitutional questions about the right of the military to participate in and criticize government policy making. Though many Americans were attracted by the prospect of a crusade against China or even the Soviet Union, especially because continuing the limited war in Korea promised only increased costs and more deaths for limited returns, Truman was not tempted. War with China would be, in the words of General Omar Bradley, chairman of the Joint Chiefs of Staff, "the wrong war, at the wrong place, at the wrong time, with the wrong enemy."

At 1:00 A.M. on April 11, 1951, Washington reporters filed into the White House newsroom for an emergency press conference. They had no idea why they had been summoned. Truman's press secretary handed out copies of an announcement that MacArthur was relieved of his command "effective at once" because he was "unable to give his whole-hearted support to the policies of the United States and the United Nations."

Within 48 hours, 125,000 telegrams poured into Washington. Letters, telegrams, and telephone calls were 20 to 1 against the president. "Impeach the little ward politician stupidity from Kansas City," said one telegram. To Hell with the Reds and Harry Truman, proclaimed a picket sign paraded in front of the White House. MacArthur returned to the United States for the first time since 1936. On April 19 he addressed Congress. Thirty million radio listeners heard him say, "Why, my soldiers asked of me, surrender military advantages to an enemy in the field? I could not answer." He concluded with an eloquent self-eulogy, " 'Old soldiers never die; they just fade away.' And like the old soldier of that ballad, I now close my military career and just fade away — an old soldier who tried to do his duty as God gave him the light to see that duty. Good-bye." As MacArthur left the floor of Congress, one senator shouted, "It's disloyal not to agree with General MacArthur!" Representative Dewey Short of Missouri said, "We have heard God speak today. God in the flesh, the voice of God."

A worried Truman held courageously to his decision. Civilian control of the military was an old, respected principle widely accepted in the United States. Gradually, calmer voices asserted themselves. MacArthur soon proved to be a poor spokesman for his own cause. He had little in common

> *For years Truman had been contemptuous of MacArthur's airs and suspicious of his political ambitions.*
> —ROBERT J. DONOVAN
> Truman biographer

with ordinary Americans and alienated the public and the press with his lofty, self-righteous manner.

In June, as the dispute over MacArthur wound down, the Chinese agreed to begin armistice negotiations in Korea. Unfortunately, the negotiations dragged on intermittently for two years while thousands more died. A major problem was that the United States did not recognize Mao's government. A peace would not be signed until Truman left office.

Meanwhile, the cold war had triggered a series of decisions by the Truman administration that would have major consequences for the future. In 1950 the United States first made a strong commitment to provide economic support for France's effort to maintain control over its colonies in Indochina (including Vietnam). Four years later, when the French

His approval ratings in public opinion polls at an all-time low, Truman decided not to seek reelection in 1952. At the Democratic convention in July, Truman introduced Adlai Stevenson, the Democratic presidential nominee, to the delegates, but during the election campaign Stevenson sought to disassociate himself from Truman.

were defeated by the Vietminh, or League for the Independence of Vietnam, led by Ho Chi Minh, the United States would feel compelled to assume an increased role in Southeast Asia.

In 1949 a new plan for an expansion of the military was developed within the National Security Council, which had been created by Truman to advise him on foreign policy. Known as NSC-68, the writers of the plan assumed that the Soviet Union intended to challenge the United States all over the world. "The Soviet Union, unlike previous aspirants to hegemony, is animated by a new fanatic faith . . . and seeks to impose its absolute authority over the rest of the world." Because the United States needed to be prepared to act anywhere in the world, the planners called for a tripling of expenditures for American military power. At first Truman did not agree, but the Korean War changed his mind. In 1950 the United States embarked on a major buildup of its military strength.

By 1952 Truman's administration was burdened with troubles. A series of petty financial scandals involved several men close to the president; typi-

The Truman home in Independence. Truman composed his memoirs, helped establish the Truman Library, and kept abreast of public affairs during the last 20 years of his life.

cally, Truman defended his cronies from critics. Newspapers referred to "the mess in Washington." McCarthy continued to denounce traitors in government. The Korean War was dragging on with no end in sight. As the 1952 elections approached, Republicans harped on Korea, communism, and corruption as issues. Truman's ratings in the polls sank to 23 percent, their lowest point.

Truman at first flirted with the idea of running for president again in 1952. A new amendment to the Constitution limited presidents to two terms, but the amendment did not apply to him. His family and friends wisely persuaded him not to make the attempt. Thinking that the Republicans would nominate Ohio's Senator Robert Taft, leader of the conservative faction and cosponsor of the unpopular Labor-Management Relations Act, Truman concluded that any reasonable Democrat would likely win in 1952. When the name of the governor of Illinois and eventual Democratic nominee, Adlai Stevenson, was first mentioned, Truman protested, "I don't believe the people of the United States are ready for an Ivy Leaguer."

After deciding that he would stand with his party and back Stevenson, Truman unwisely tried to make the Illinois governor his protégé. He attended the party convention, rallied support for Stevenson, and presented the candidate to the convention after the nomination, only to have Stevenson claim that he was indebted to no one for his nomination. He repeatedly invited Stevenson to Washington to discuss the campaign, but the candidate declined. Stevenson also replaced the head of the Democratic Committee with a friend of his without first informing Truman. It appeared that the last thing Stevenson wanted was the support of the unpopular Truman.

The Republicans overlooked Taft and nominated Dwight David Eisenhower, hero of World War II. Truman felt betrayed; he had believed that he and Eisenhower were Democratic colleagues and friends. Eisenhower's easy, open, friendly manner made Truman appear combative, crusty, and aggressive by comparison. Eisenhower's campaign was highly critical of Truman. The two men became increasingly hostile.

Truman developed a joke about the Republican initials, GOP, which, he said, did not stand for Grand Old Party, as people thought, but for the "Generals' Own Party." In addition to Eisenhower, there were General MacArthur, General Motors, and General Electric, but "general welfare is with the corporals and the privates in the Democratic Party." Eisenhower won a resounding victory in 1952. Between the election and the inauguration, the two men came together only once for a formal meeting. On the day of the inauguration they treated each other coldly and resentfully.

More than 5,000 people showed up at Union Station in Washington to see the Trumans off to Missouri. In Independence, they were welcomed by another crowd of about 5,000. He wrote in his diary, "Mrs. T and I were overcome. It was the pay-off for thirty years of hell and hard work."

Truman lived for almost 20 years after he left the presidency. Only Herbert Hoover lived longer as a

Four U.S. presidents were photographed together at the November 18, 1961, funeral of Sam Rayburn, longtime Speaker of the House of Representatives. From left to right are John Kennedy, Lyndon Johnson (who became president on the death of Kennedy in November 1963), Eisenhower, and Truman.

former president. Truman busied himself with family, friends, work on his memoirs, and travel. He was especially pleased about the construction of the Truman Library in Independence, and for years he visited the library every day. His daughter says that he continued to read two newspapers a day and kept up with public events right up until the end of his life. On December 26, 1972, he died in a Kansas City hospital. He was buried in the courtyard of the Truman Library.

In many ways, Harry S. Truman seemed an unlikely leader of the United States at midcentury. Unpretentious, provincial, and combative, he became president despite his relatively ordinary origins and lack of education. At the very moment when the energy of the atom was harnessed and when the United States achieved world power, Truman

Truman continued to support the Democratic party after his retirement from office. He is shown here at a Democratic fund-raiser in 1954.

brought into the highest councils of government a commonsense, pragmatic style of American democracy.

Spencer Tracy, in the movie *A Guy Named Joe*, says, "Everything is going to be prettier, you're going to have no more bad dreams, you're going to have all the things people have . . . ." Americans after World War II optimistically pursued the good life in a prosperous new society. Veterans went to college, graduated, and sought jobs in expanding corporate America. As one graduate said, "I know AT&T might not be very exciting, but there will always be an AT&T."

Within five years after the war ended, American technology perfected the automatic car transmission, the ballpoint pen, the electric clothes dryer, the automatic garbage disposal unit, and the long-

Truman walks the streets of Independence shortly after his return there from Washington. He spent the early days of his retirement working on his *Memoirs*, which were published in 1955.

playing record. New "wonder" fibers, such as nylon and vinyl, transformed clothing, floors, and much more. By 1953, when Truman left office, one half of American homes had television sets. New antibiotics such as penicillin and the -mycin drugs attacked such dread communicable diseases as tuberculosis and syphilis.

Truman seemed out of place in the new affluence. He was neither comfortable nor effective on television, and he did not speak the language of modern public relations and the consumer culture. He and Bess never bought many things and seemed comfortable and happy with their modest life-style.

In many of the ways that mattered most, however, Truman was very much a man of his age. He grew up with America in the 20th century and was prepared for life and leadership in a new technological era. He knew about modern war from his days as a veteran. In Kansas City he became familiar with planning for modern automobile and air transportation, and in the Senate he learned the ways of

Bess Truman (top center) is escorted to the grave of her husband. Truman died on December 20, 1972, and was buried in the courtyard of the Truman Library in Independence, Missouri.

Although Truman was unpopular and underestimated while in office, his reputation has since risen. The scandals and cover-ups of Richard Nixon's administration during the early 1970s created a nostalgia for Truman's forthright, plainspoken style, and historians have ranked Truman as a near-great president, comparable in stature to Theodore Roosevelt and Andrew Jackson.

modern bureaucracy and government. He ushered in the nuclear age with confidence and an awareness of the responsibilities of power.

In 1962 a poll of American historians ranked Truman in the "near-great" category along with such presidents as Andrew Jackson and Theodore Roosevelt. He warranted high ranking because of his leadership during the many extreme foreign crises he faced. Confronting new and dangerous problems, he led the country through difficult times and constructed a group of policies that would guide the nation long into the future.

Truman's style — that of a self-educated county courthouse politician — made him easy to underestimate. But such men as Dean Acheson and George Marshall saw through the style, proclaiming him a man for whom it was an honor to work. In time, his reputation improved in the country as a whole. Gradually, Americans became more appreciative of the difficult situations he faced and of the courage with which he confronted the modern age.

Further Reading

Donovan, Robert J. *Conflict and Crisis.* New York: Norton, 1977.

———. *Tumultuous Years.* New York: Norton, 1982.

Ferrell, Robert H. *Dear Bess: The Letters from Harry to Bess Truman, 1910–1959.* New York: Norton, 1983.

———. *Harry S. Truman and the Modern American Presidency.* Boston: Little, Brown, 1982.

———. *Off the Record.* New York: Penguin, 1980.

Jenkins, Roy. *Truman.* New York: Harper & Row, 1986.

Miller, Merle. *Plain Speaking.* New York: G. P. Putnam's Sons, 1982.

Miller, Richard Lawrence. *Truman: The Rise to Power.* New York: McGraw-Hill, 1985.

Truman, Margaret. *Bess W. Truman.* New York: Macmillan, 1986.

Chronology

May 8, 1884	Born Harry S. Truman in Lamar, Missouri
1917–19	Serves in U.S. Army during World War I
1922	Elected judge of eastern part of Jackson County
1934–44	Serves as Democratic senator from Missouri
Dec. 8, 1941	United States enters World War II
1944	Truman selected as Franklin Roosevelt's presidential running mate
Feb. 1945	Yalta Conference held
April 12, 1945	Roosevelt dies; Truman sworn in as president
April 23, 1945	Truman meets with Soviet foreign minister Molotov
April 25–May 1945	United Nations conference convenes in San Francisco
May 8, 1945	Germany surrenders
July 15, 1945	Potsdam Conference begins
July 16, 1945	First successful U.S. atomic bomb test
Aug. 6, 1945	Atomic bomb dropped on Hiroshima
Aug. 9, 1945	Atomic bomb dropped on Nagasaki
Sept. 2, 1945	Japan surrenders
1946	Industrial and housing problems trouble the United States; food and fuel shortages cripple Europe; civil war breaks out in China
Feb. 26, 1947	National Security Act passed
March 12, 1947	Truman Doctrine introduced
June 9, 1947	Marshall Plan introduced
May 1948	The United States recognizes independent state of Israel
1948	Berlin airlift begins
Nov. 1948	Truman wins reelection
Jan. 9, 1949	Truman announces Fair Deal plan
April 4, 1949	International agreement establishes foundations of NATO
Oct. 1949	The United States learns of Soviet atomic bomb test
June 24, 1950	Korean War begins
June 1951	Stable front established at 38th parallel; armistice negotiations begin
1952	Truman decides not to seek reelection; Dwight D. Eisenhower elected president
1955	Publishes his *Memoirs*
1962	Historians rank Truman with Andrew Jackson and Theodore Roosevelt as "near-great" president
Dec. 26, 1972	Harry S. Truman dies in Kansas City hospital

Index

J. Perry Leavell, Jr., teaches American history at Drew University. He has written on Theodore Roosevelt and on the development of democracy in the United States. He is also the author of *Woodrow Wilson* in the Chelsea House series *World Leaders   Past & Present.*

Arthur M. Schlesinger, jr., taught history at Harvard for many years and is currently Albert Schweitzer Professor of the Humanities at City University of New York. He is the author of numerous highly praised works in American history and has twice been awarded the Pulitzer Prize. He served in the White House as special assistant to Presidents Kennedy and Johnson.

PICTURE CREDITS

AP/Wide World Photos: pp. 15, 16, 43, 57, 74, 76, 79, 83, 90, 92, 94, 104, 105; Dorothea Lange, Library of Congress: pp. 48, 90; Harry S. Truman Library: pp. 31, 33, 37; Library of Congress: p. 60; National Archives: pp. 12, 14, 18, 20, 22, 29, 30, 32, 34, 35, 38, 41, 42, 45, 50, 56, 59, 62, 63, 68, 69, 82, 84, 96, 101, 102, 107; UPI/Bettmann: pp. 17, 19, 21, 23, 25, 27, 28, 52, 58, 61, 64, 65, 66, 67, 70, 78, 85, 86, 87, 88, 95, 97, 100, 103, 106.